Fly Again

I WANT YOU TO LIVE

ANNETTE TIDBALL

Fly Again

Cover Art by Simon Dewey

Quantity sales special discounts are available on quantity purchases by corporations, associations, and others. For details, contact the publisher at the address above.

Orders by U.S. trade bookstores and wholesalers. Email info@ BeyondPublishing.net

The Author can be reached directly BeyondPublishing.net/ AuthorAnnetteTidball

Manufactured and printed in the United States of America distributed globally by BeyondPublishing.net

New York | Los Angeles | London | Sydney

ISBN Hardcover: 978-1-949873-91-7

ISBN Softcover: 978-1-947256-39-2

Endorsements

Amberly Rae Neilson *"A real devastating, yet inspirational story or guide on heartbreak, love, tragic loss and how to overcome one's trials in the face of adversity. It is definitely a must read."*

Craig Neilson - *"Such a great book with amazing life experiences and lessons that will give any reader 'the feels'. It would be hard to find someone that couldn't relate in some way to this book regardless of age, gender, or background. Pick it up and read it, you won't regret it!"*

Don Hughes- *"A book that will open doors in your being, doors that will bring satisfying memories of times past and open up a vision of life full of love and warm relationships. What can be instead of what has been. A healing journey of the soul to reflect on life and gain what might have been lost through trouble and tragedy."*

Savannah Tilley- *"Fly Again is a wonderfully written book full of love and a beautiful message to keep moving forward even after tragedy strikes. It's so raw and real and will bring everyone who reads it to tears."*

Kevin Tidball - *"Direct. Vulnerable. Fabulous read. Captivating. Heart warming. Fly Again is one of the most powerful books I have read in years. Annette shares and shows her passion for developing lasting and enduring relationships. Fly Again is simple but tasteful, you won't be able to put the book down."*

Maile Tilley - *"While reading my Mom's book, the grief and anguish I felt as a 6 year-old girl came back. After years of suppressed heartache, this beautiful book acted as a tool to help me overcome and comprehend our sudden tragic experience. After completing the book I truly understand what my mom endured. Overcome by my own struggles, I failed to notice her continuous trials of faith. My mother is a strong, faithful, and obedient woman which is evident in this must-read book ;) "*

Magi Tidball - *"I absolutely loved it. The love and emotion that she put into writing that book really shows as you read it. I especially enjoyed the end of each chapter where she put the little tips, because they really helped me to ponder about what happened in the previous chapter and it got me thinking about how I could apply those things in my life. I think overall she did a wonderful job."*

Sandy Woodhead - *"Annette's captivating words will make you feel the butterflies, hear the sweetness and sense the gentleness of a truly magical love. Fly Again is an inspiring true story of love, loss & acceptance that guides you with simple reminders of how mindset, trust & faith grant you the choices to direct your life towards your dreams."*

Rob Woodhead - *"Captivating and enthralling. Annette's way of storytelling is like talking to a best friend. It's one of those books you just can't put down. I am always grateful when someone writes their true self and honest struggles. She is inspirational and the book is a must read for everyone."*

Liz Woodruff - *"What Annette experienced is a traumatic pain no one should have to go through, but the incredible light and hope she shares is something we all need to hear. She is one of the most inspiring women I have ever met. She is strong, faithful, steadfast, and empowering to all those she comes in contact with. This story is so powerful, moving, and timely. We live in a time in this world when the message that God exists; that there is life after death; that family members look out for us even after they've passed on from this life; and most importantly that we are never alone no matter what we are going through is so important. We need hope and we need love; this book delivers both."*

Bruce Riopelle - *"An amazing witness to love, heartache, hope and faith."*

Cathy Butts - *"I feel the peace exposed in this autobiography."*

Cheryl Tilley - *"It makes me feel really good about life that some greater positivity, that can be shared, has come from a huge loss. Brye and (Annette) are still sharing the love and teaching us earthlings the greatest of lessons. Thanks for your bravery. "*

Mark Tilley - *"From a brother's perspective...what those two had was amazing. I have never seen my brother smile with love like he did with her and the girls. My girls ask, 'What was Uncle Brian like?' I just show them a picture and say, 'Like that.' Annette made my brother smile and so did his girls. Annette is awesome. I love her and thank her for her story."*

Russ McLean - *"With Annette's new book, I simply sat back, took a deep breath and admired what I had just read, all-the-while trying to comprehend even a portion of her journey. If there ever was a woman who demonstrates how to "become the Truest, Purest You", it is Annette. Her story is unique, yet universal, it is personal yet profoundly human. Reading her experience reminds a person of the importance, the absolute necessity to connect with "Someone greater than us, [someone], willing to help us in our journey, call it the Universe, I call it God."*

Annette is an inspiration to those who find themselves lost through either no fault of their own or through their own experience. Annette's story is pure and beautiful, because it is about love, about bonding, about eternity, about decisions, about trust, about being vulnerable and humble. Annette let's all of us see that if we lean not unto our own understanding, but trust to recognize and understand the Spirit's sweet whisperings within our soul, we too can overcome, learn and progress. This is a beautiful book, written by a very beautiful person. Well done Annette and thank you for laying your vulnerability of soul on these pages."

Marni Laveck - *"In this book Annette shows the profound impact that choices have on our lives. Read, learn and grow."*

Karen Zahacy - *"This is a captivating story of love, perseverance, and friendship. Annette's life embodies hope and the human spirit."*

Kristie Garber - *"Compelling and honest, Annette's story details her journey through shattering loss of true love and God's surprising design to rebuild her life. It provides inspiration to anyone who has struggled to maintain faith and triumph over bewildering adversity."*

Dedication

I dedicate this book to my late husband, Brian. He unknowingly planted seeds inside my heart. Seeds of gratitude, gentleness, humility, authenticity, strength, and the deepest, truest form of love. He knew my great worth before I ever did. He was an exceptional husband, father, and friend. To me, he was near perfect. With him, I have an enlightened knowledge of things to come. Without him, this story would not be.

I dedicate this book to all of my children. To those who experienced the most, Amberly, Savannah, Maile, and Paige. They have each shared the same journey on their own paths. They opened my eyes to see beyond the veil. To my gentle children who had no idea why I was so messed up, Jade and Braden. Each of them are so individually strong in their own right. They make me proud every single day.

I dedicate this book to Kevin. He is my rock. He believes in me. He encourages me. He loves me with an unjealous love. His strength got me through the most difficult years of my life. Without him, I also would have a different story to tell. He made my life fun again. He showed me new adventures don't replace the old, they just enhance them. He made me believe I could love again, no matter how the world judged me.

I would show such ingratitude if I did not thank my Heavenly Father and his son, Jesus Christ, for veiling me in their love. We truly wrote this book together. They know me better than I know myself. They knew I would come out on the other side a better, stronger woman. A woman who could help others with her story.

And lastly, I dedicate this book to all of my trials, without which I would never have become frustrated and mad enough to change the effects of my past, to trust the process, or become strong enough to write. Thank you for knowing that you would be the elements to my success. I didn't like you then, I probably won't like you in the future, but I can appreciate you in this moment.

Acknowledgements

There are so many people to thank. So many caring hearts and generous hands. I thank all of you. I realize there are many who worked behind the scenes and did much for me and my girls in ways I may never know. My heart is grateful. My family is grateful.

Thank you firstly to Rita and John Tilley for creating a beautiful, independent son. He became such a remarkable human being and a man whom I was so honored to be married to.

To the Church of Jesus Christ of Latter-Day Saints, and the truly inspired church it is with all it's organizations: the women's organization of the Relief Society and it's wonderful sisterhood, the men's organization of brothers, the sweet youth in the Young Men and Young Women's program and the innocent children in the Primary, all of you work so diligently in serving the Lord, "willingly to mourn with those who mourn...and comfort those in need of comfort." (Mosiah 18:9) Indeed, you did mourn with us and comfort us in our greatest time of need.

To Brian's wonderful family members who supported me during the time of the accident and beyond: Mark Tilley, Cheryl Tilley, Donna Tilley, Keri and Jamie Emin, Kim Tilley, Keith and Allyson Tilley, Kent Tilley, Judy Unwin-Tilley, Scott and Deidre Tilley, Steve Tilley, Rainer and Claudia Salomaa, Sonja Salomaa, Diana Salomaa, Henry Dembicki, Nigel Dembicki, Geoff Dembicki, Anita Silvester.

To Kevin's family who accepted me and all the new excitement that came with me and my girls, thank you for opening your hearts up to a new daughter/sister/auntie and new grandchildren/nieces/cousins: Donna and Dennis Tidball, Marcie and Mike Sera, Hayley and McKay Sera, Cameron and Sara Tidball, Madison, Cooper, Dexter and Spencer Tidball, Kelsey Sharpe, Jake, Abbey and Parker Oviatt.

Many thanks go to all of those wonderful friends who came and served me by giving Priesthood blessings, and picking up my girls, bringing meals, taking notes, helping to prepare Brian's memorial, sweeping and mopping my floor, painting toe-nails, buying pilot Build-a-bears, cutting our grass, helping with school supplies, the list is long. And thank you to the many many wonderful human beings who donated to the Tilley girls' fund when we so desperately needed it.

Friends

Kristie Garber - for being my best friend through all of the ups and downs over the years
Al Garber - sorting out all my legal issues
Liz and Ron Woodruff - for being remarkable, helpful, and supportive
Suzy and Albert James - staying by my side, blessings and friendship
Karen Wilde and Justin - being there every step of the way during his passing and assisting me in planning the funeral
Jordan and Jennifer Woodruff - for being an amazing home teacher who cared
Darin and Terri Pitcher, Talia,Tyson and Talon - for being friends from before, during and after Brian in my life
Laura Lane - how we journeyed our own sad paths together, and for the final push to get started on my book
Nadine Sturko - understanding my pain, doing all you could as Relief Society President
Kevin Sauvé - for the revealing blessing
Chris Mack (and wife Eva Mack) - being so compassionate and playing Amazing Grace at Brian's memorial
Ryan and Tanya Handley - for reconnecting just before the accident and being great friends ever since
Lael Horne - for bringing me the deli platter when I was sick of lasagne!
Tammy Jones for staying the night and being a great friend over the years
Simon Dewey - for creating such a touching cover
Tracy and Darrell Johnston - being the best neighbours and someone I could run to after I heard the news
Marie von Reitmyer - our Doula who helped bring our little girls into the world
Al Shaw - for connecting with Brian -like young kids when talking about flying

Lesley Chaisson - for making my incredible wedding dress based off a picture and bridesmaid dresses in record time
Marni and Bryce Laveck - for planning such a speedy wedding and retrieving Brian's body for us
Chris Marusiak - therapy after the accident
Marianne Edwards- taking my girls out to spend time with yours
Nancy Hartmier- 'supervising' Brian and I those many years ago
Iain Reynolds - for being such a great friend to Brian
Sandy Woodhead and Rob Woodhead - for going through copious pictures and choosing the best ones
Karen James - choosing those final pictures to add
Dan "the Man" - who drove the Loomis truck, whose last name I cannot find but who insisted I be late for my wedding by stopping to get lemonade at a child's lemonade stand
Doug and Rachel Atwood - for being the Bishop who stressed Brian out that I wasn't coming
Ida and Norm Link
Dennis and Cari Johnson
Gerry Hippard
Rachel and Aaron Johnson
Jared and Kristi Pitcher
James Wood
Tara Jones
Raf and Ami Bustamante
Anthony and Natalie Hoy
Vicky and JD Copland
Phyllis Snider (Scamper)
Our Homeless friends, some of whom have since passed - for making dating Brian fun downtown

Can-West Corporate Air Charters/Airborne

Jim Vomastic - thanks for the visit and support
Terris Dods- thank you for such a beautiful speech at Brian's memorial, and being a friend
Rob Elford
Kyle Thorsell

Conair

Andrew Robertson - thank you for being a good friend to Brian and for being there after the crash
Tony Quo Vadis
Andrea Strain Gray
Dennis Graham
Cindy Malette
Greg McMaster

NAV CANADA/B.C. Forest Service/Canadian Fallen Firefighters Foundation

Jeff Berry
Jamie Brown
Bob Kirkpatrick
Doug Wylie
Bruce Rushton

Eden North and Skydivers

George Marshall
Lyle and Cathy Waddell @ Eden North - for giving Brian a job flying skydivers

Government

The Rt. Hon. Stephen Harper, Prime Minister of Canada and his wife Laureen Harper
Gordon Campbell Premier of British Columbia
Dana Hayden Deputy Minister -British Columbia Ministry of Forests and Range

Of course, a thank you to the bird dog pilot who filmed the crash and could provide answers, the first responders who risked their lives to put out Brian's fire, and those on foot who went to see if there were any survivors, and to the firemen from all over Canada who felt the loss and always made us feel like we were part of the firefighter family.

To all of you whose names are not here, my gratitude is heartfelt. Thank you.

Why I Wrote This Book

You know those moments when you feel like there have been so many trials and you'd just like to come up for air? Those moments when you need a break? Just let me have one moment to catch my breath before I get plunged into the deep dark waters again. Yeah, those moments. I know those moments. Who doesn't? Don't we all have life events that we have to endure? Moments in time that shape us?

I can't be the only one who has also heard the words, "find your purpose", or "live your purpose"! Then I quietly cried inside feeling my purpose was not as grandiose as the person who said it. My purposes have been raising 6 wonderful children, and all the cooking, cleaning and never-ending laundry that came with that! I couldn't see that I had any extraordinary purpose, and yet I yearned to know what it could possibly be. How could I make a difference in the lives of others, outside of my own home?

I pled with the Lord to know what more was there to my life? The trials seemed to bury me. The heaviness like a thick suffocating blanket. As soon as I thought we were out of it, a new one would come and then another and another. I couldn't seem to catch my breath. I'd like to say that I was in total control of my thoughts in those moments, but no, I wasn't. My spirit was getting so tired, I felt so overwhelmed. And being mad at God was not helping. In fact, when you pray all day with anger in your heart, the Spirit leaves and you feel more empty.

My focus changed. I asked Him to forgive me for being angry. After all, this life is a place of learning, not a smooth and easy ride. Instead of asking for my burdens to be taken away I began to pray for them to feel lighter. I began asking what I could do to make things better. I began asking, "What is my next step?" And then I would listen.

I went forward with faith, expecting an answer and being prepared to go and do it. (I had done many hard things with His help before, so why had I forgotten that?) The answer came. It was most unexpected. (His answers usually are for me).

"Write a book."

Ummm, what was that? "Pardon?"

"Write a book."

No matter what my question was, whether it was how to get enough money for a new range, (my husband had lost his job and we hadn't had a working oven, or stove for six months), or how to find more purpose in my life, (I had been raising kids for over 20 years and I was ready for something more). The answer was quiet and simple. "Write a book."

Now, this was quite interesting to me. My close friends growing up had known of my life's challenges then and had told me I should write a book. And over the last few years my girlfriend, Laura Lane and author of *Two Mother's, One Prayer*, had also encouraged me to write a book.

I had been at a yoga educational class one weekend and was so focused on tuning in to the Lord and myself, which, yes, I know is not, and was not the typical yoga spiritual journey, but if you know me at all, I am a determined woman who likes to do things my way. And my way consisted of finding out who I really am. Who was I meant to be? And what was God's plan for me?

That night I sat down at the computer and wrote until the early morning. I started at the beginning of my existence here on earth up until my soulmate came into my life. Over time I continued to add to my story with much vigor. But I couldn't write about Brian. I couldn't write about how wonderful life with him was. It felt like I couldn't remember. I was in a heavy place. Trials were like unwanted presents stacked all around me. Not being able to see clearly, all I could remember was the pain and heartache. So, my book went on hold.

Burdens were still all around me. I was still working on my anger with God issues. And I was sad. Eventually, with continued persistence, my shoulders started to feel lighter. Again, I prayed for answers to...well, anything, and again I heard, "Write your book."

This time, I fell to my knees. I really repented of not trusting Him, of blaming Him, of being angry...I returned with full focus to living my life the way I used to, a life where I felt the Spirit of God daily. I made the changes I needed to make to clean out the weeds I had let grow rampant in my brain. I read, I prayed, I fasted, I served.

One day it became very clear to me that all the trials, the heartache and the life's challenges I had experienced, had led me to this exact moment in my life. My heart felt warm and peaceful. I knew I had to finish my book. I knew I needed to share with others my story of Brian. So, I got to work. Loving memories of our time together came flooding back. Pictures, letters, and cards resurfaced.

Each day I fervently asked for His help. I knew if this is what He wanted, if this was the reason for all I had gone through, if I was supposed to help even one person know they can make it, that there is hope for them too, I needed His help. He knew who needed my book and my words better than me. So, we went to work. I would type and vent and be frustrated on the pages, only to hear a quiet voice say, "Okay, now erase that." And I would begin again. Every sentence was guided.

Mysteriously, serendipitously, or from a heavenly source, you can be the judge. But there were moments during the most painful time of my life, when a gentle voice would say, remember this, you'll need to recall this later on. Moments in my past when a random picture was taken, and then found for use in this book. I have never been one to take pictures... who takes a picture of an Alphaghetti love note? And better yet, who keeps such a thing? Us. Apparently.

My husband saw me crying those big ugly cry face cries and said, "Now what's wrong with you?" (I had been crying a lot when things were so difficult) I surprised him when I stammered, "I'm just so grateful! My trials actually do have a purpose and I love the way that I am feeling right now!"

Thank you, dear reader. Thank you for being the reason I went through the hardest days of my life. Thank you for giving me more purpose in my life, that my trials weren't for nothing. Thank you for allowing me to share what I have been through, what I know to be true and how I managed to be happy again. You are the reason for this book. You are the reason I was supposed to rise above and Fly Again.

Table of Contents

Introduction

Hi! Let me introduce myself. My name is Annette. I'm older than you think, but I like to keep you guessing. I am short, but can curl up just fine in small spaces. I colour my hair, and when I paint my toes, I like purple, yet blue is my favourite colour... interesting. Welcome to *Fly Again*. Thank you for buying/reading my book. I wrote this story to help you, and while writing this story, it also helped me. Reading old journal entries was almost like reliving much of it and very therapeutic.

I began writing my first version of this when I was entering a dark stage in my life. (Did you know that you can be put on hold when you call a suicide help line? Yup. It happened to me. "We're sorry all agents are currently unavailable.") When I picked myself up again, I was a better woman, and I had done the necessary work to be able to share this with you. (Plus, the first version was pretty dreary and sad, and who wants to read that to feel uplifted?!) So, I stood up tall, wiped myself off, strengthened myself, and now, I bring you... me. I've always been here, I just never realized *I* had the power to find me.

While writing this, it felt like a blog or a journal entry. It's a frightening thing to let people in, but I am. I'm letting you into my world, my experience. I hope you will try my shoes on and walk a mile with me. Maybe we have some commonalities in our stories, and maybe you've never experienced anything like what you're about to read. That's okay. Let's just be kind humans together. If you open up your heart, you may feel the ups and downs of my journey, too. You may think, "Woah, I get her!" And if you don't, that's okay.

There are three elements to this book: the main story, the questions, and the tips. Firstly, you may wish to read the story all the way through. (That's what I would do personally, because this is an amazing story, and who wouldn't want to read it until the end? Just saying...) Secondly, there may be times that you need a little emotional break. No problem, continue with the questions for some not so serious self-analysis. Thirdly, you may wish to pop over to the tips section, where I give some pointers on what made life so amazing, how I made it through, and how I dealt with the unexpected. And you may find that you read it again and again, differently each time.

I'm not here to change your life, but I'd like to. I'm not here to tell you how and what you should feel, but you may find it shifting after you read this. I'd like to be the one who helps you rise above and take your life to the next step. Whatever you do with your life, may this be helpful. Even though I don't know you and I may never meet you, I wrote this book for you. Believe me, I prayerfully did.

Chapter 1

The Prep

I was married to a man who didn't love me, and I really had no idea what real love looked like. I grew up in what is now, unfortunately, the new norm: a very dysfunctional family. I met David* when I was 20, shortly after becoming a member of the Church of Jesus Christ of Latter -Day Saints and a very disconcerted young girl. I hadn't been taught to cherish myself as a daughter of God, so I confused lust with love. Soon, I found myself pregnant and asking a reluctant David to marry me. I wasn't done dating. I knew he wasn't the one for me, but my own choices have consequences. He said his bishop suggested we put our baby up for adoption. My inner momma voice vehemently said, "No way!" I had our beautiful daughter, Amberly, at 21.

We each wanted different things. I wanted someone I could talk to about anything and everything. I wanted a best friend. A man I could trust, a man I loved to spend time with, who also loved spending time with me, doing things we both enjoyed. I wanted my little girl to have an amazing father who stayed and played with her, who wanted to teach her how to tie her shoes and throw a baseball. I wanted a husband I could run and kiss at the door when he came home.

One day, David was confronted with a choice. He wanted to live a different way, without the church. He wanted to have a different life, with another person, not with us. I found myself alone, a single mom, with no family support; just my little girl, the church, and me.

As with all the difficult times in my life, my heart was broken again. More than anything, I wanted to have a happy, loving family. I grew up watching shows with happy families. I wanted my version of a happy family. Ever since I was a little girl, I dreamt of being a mom. Yes, I had other dreams, but I wanted so badly to be a mommy, and now, I had to find a way to take care of the two of us. I hated that I had to take her to daycare, and she hated it, too. I simultaneously applied for school and a job at a law firm.

I didn't like being alone. I had no family I could talk to. I had no brothers or sisters, nor had I yet found my tribe. I had difficulty connecting to true friends who didn't delight in mocking me behind my back. Being walked out on was very hard, and it felt like I was grieving. The divorce was not terrible, but full of heartache. And I was very much alone. I cried a lot. She cried a lot. If David was in the basement, Amberly would crouch down and shout to him through the heating vent on the floor. The morning after he left, she couldn't find him, so she did just that— calling for Daddy, who wouldn't come back. My four-year-old sweetheart was heartbroken, too.

Things started to take new form. I took charge of our spiritual progression. It wasn't ideal, but I do remember appreciating our scripture and prayer times and how we enjoyed the Sabbath day. Because she was so little, we would play with homemade play-dough, making our scripture stories come alive. Singing, dancing, and story time held deeper meaning, just the two of us. I held her so close. Time with her was precious.

Our burdens felt lighter, and I found myself smiling again. I would marvel at a single, beautiful snowflake melting on the sleeve of my black jacket. I would listen more at work and speak less. I would sing in the mailroom. I watched my tongue and spoke no guile.

My bishop at the time asked me a contemplative question. "Do you want to be married to David? Or do you want to be married?" Deep inside, I knew the answer. He did, too. My bishop suggested that I act as though I was preparing to get married. Inspired counsel? In retrospect, yes, it was. I remember sitting down and writing a list of all the traits I wanted in my future husband: how I wanted him to look, to speak, and to treat me. What his accomplishments were. He had to be trustworthy, sincere, fun to be with, appreciate me, and love both my daughter and me fully and deeply. We were a package deal. I wrote that he had to have a great smile with straight teeth, tall, and good-looking, with a cute bum! You bet. I wrote it all.

I took this list and set it beside me. I began my usual prayer, then opened my eyes and literally read the entire list to my Heavenly Father. If a man like this existed, and it was in the plans of my life to be married to him, then the Creator of the Universe knew where he was and how to get him to me.

I began believing I would be married. To *whom*, I had absolutely no idea, I just had unwavering faith in what I had been counseled. I recall scanning the church on Sundays and the grocery store thinking, "Is it him? Could it be him? Will he be old? A single dad?" That makes me smile thinking back.

I gazed around my home and thought, *If I were to be married right now, what would I change?* I did not like my dishes; I realize that seems rather odd, but I wanted new ones. I ventured out to Ikea and bought myself pretty new dishes for my future with *a new husband*. (Faith is an action word, after all.)

In a priesthood blessing, I was counseled to keep a positive mind and attitude. So, I did. I really did. Things were tough, but I kept my head up. I got offered a job at the law firm the exact same day I was accepted into college. My choice here is significant. I chose the job to take care of the immediate needs of my preschooler. And that is how I met *him*.

How Are You Prepping for a Better Life?

1). When faced with a trial, what do you do?

a). I stay in bed, mope, and cry as much as possible.

b). I cry for a bit, stop thinking about it, and keep going.

c). I see what can be learned and move forward with faith that things will get better.

2). When loved ones hurt you, what do you do?

a). I talk nasty about them to anyone who will listen, then feel ugly inside and not know why.

b). I endlessly write in my journal, put a smile on for the world, and pretend everything is alright.

c). I write a letter of forgiveness to them they will never see and move onward and upward, knowing I still have worth.

3). If someone gives you advice you don't agree with, what do you do?

a). I do nothing. They don't know what they are talking about. I just keep doing things the way I've always done them, but expecting change to happen.

b). I become angry inside, shut them out, talk down about them, and do the opposite, just in spite.

c). I thoughtfully consider the counsel, weigh the options (maybe even argue at first), and either pray to get an answer or go with my 'gut' feeling.

TIPS

1). **When you are prepared, you have nothing to fear!**

Before David left me, I could feel a shift in the atmosphere around him and our home. Knowing I didn't have all the answers, I prayed and asked what to expect. Answers came. Hard answers. At first, I was very fearful of letting go and what that would look like. Once I did, and I trusted that God/our Creator knew all things and also wanted me to be happy. I leaned on that hope and trust.

You can ask what to expect from God/the Great Creator/the Universe. Be prepared that you may not hear what you want to hear. But, if and when you do, be ready to do something about it! Don't ask the questions without being willing to do the work.

2). **Clean out your closet!**

Saying goodbye to someone or something can be like cleaning out your closet. Going through your old, used, and sometimes even the never-been-worn clothes with the tags still on is not only a liberating feeling, it creates space. Breathing space. You are allowing the universe room to bring you something better. Something that fits and looks great in your *now* life, not the life from five years ago.

Finally, letting go of a loved one who broke my heart, who didn't want to be there, was like taking a big breath of fresh air.

3). **Count your blessings!**

Create a "blessings" journal. Not a venting journal. A journal you would never be ashamed of if someone read it. (Don't worry, I have some of those venting journals, too, which reminds me...I should go burn those!) When I noticed the beauty in a snowflake, I was showing the Universe/God how appreciative I was that something so small was made to be so beautiful, even if only for a moment. This allowed me to believe that if so much care and attention was put into creating an exquisite snowflake that was gone in an instant on my sleeve, how much more exquisite was I?

4). **Look forward to a brighter future!**

Keep the image of your future in your mind, in your excitement, in your energy. I knew how I wanted to be loved. I knew when things were over with David that I wanted to be married again. I became excited. I acted as though I was to be married soon, buying new dishes and organizing my house. I would think, *If I were getting married next month, what would I change right now?* This kept my energy and hopes up.

5). **Trust in the timing!**

All good things come to those who (actively) wait. If you're faithful and believing...you see your dream, you feel it, and you keep getting up each time you lose focus. If you know you are doing your best to prepare for your future and if you have faith it will come - it *will* come. It will come when you are ready. It will come when all other circumstances are aligned. Because, like the saying goes, when preparation and opportunity meet, you will find success.

** Name has been changed*

Chapter 2

The Miracle

It was the beginning of February. My divorce was almost final. I was in the dark basement of a beautiful historic CIBC building downtown, depositing some cheques for the firm. (Brian's version of this story is not the same as mine.) I heard clicking on the stairs, and I assumed it was a woman in heels. I was surprised to look up to see cycling shoes, mismatched cycling socks, black MEC fleece pants, a bright yellow jacket, trendy black-rimmed glasses, and brown curly hair spilling through the spaces in his helmet. He was rummaging through his worn courier bag slung over his shoulder and speaking loudly into an equally loud radio perched upon his strap. I didn't think he had noticed me. I noticed him. My heart uncontrollably fluttered. He was cute. But I also thought he was very rude to be so loud and oblivious to everyone else in line. I looked down at my feet, which were suddenly the most interesting things to me at that moment.

I had been waiting for some time at the front of the line when this young (tall, dark, and handsome) man walked in. Corresponding with my previous inclination that he was rude, he avoided the end of the line and made his way straight to the teller! (Unbeknownst to me, couriers had this luxury at many of their stops, in order to keep up with their timely deliveries.) The teller must have seen my dropped jaw, because she quickly introduced us as I took my turn at the teller beside him. She called him Barry, and he quickly corrected her, “My name's not Barry. You know me. I've worked with your husband before. My name is Brian.” (This is one of the parts Brian disputes). The teller looked somewhat embarrassed. She corrected herself and re-introduced us. He was in a disgruntled mood that day, I guess. I extended my hand, and he ignored it. (Here's the second part he disputes: he denies that he would have ever been so rude as to not take my hand. Okay, so not a great first impression.)

This first abrupt encounter could have tarnished my opinion of Brian, but I soon found out he had a meekness and gentleness to him. We were both immediately awakened by our introduction. He said it was love at first sight, and that he couldn't stop thinking about me. I definitely couldn't stop thinking about him. He was oddly refreshing to me.

One crisp morning, he saw me purposefully walking from my bus stop to work. He had a small, hot coffee in one hand and pushed his bike along with the other. Soon, we were in perfect, unified cadence. A sign of a perfect union to come. He began to ask me some very 'I want to get to know you questions' right from the start. (This man wasted no time!) I was thrilled to have such an attractive and intriguing man taking the time to get to know me. My heart felt warm. This was so comfortable. I needed to be honest with him and not lead him astray about my current life situation. I frankly told him: “I need to be honest with you. I am not yet divorced, and I have a daughter.” I was afraid he would run away, but he did not. He didn't even flinch! Instead, his words were sweet and authentic. When he spoke, I felt— well, it's very odd to describe — I felt warm inside. His words felt rich and warm to my soul. He asked my daughter's name and how old she was. He was genuinely interested and not at all worried or intimidated. I felt the sincerity of his words when he spoke. I was even more intrigued. What kind of man would actually be interested in my existing family life? He was so sincere. I knew I had never met anyone like him before. I didn't know anyone like him existed.

Brian quickly learned my bus schedule and conveniently managed to meet me as soon as I hopped off my bus. Walking beside him felt natural. Talking with him was easy. My hidden secrets seemed to simply slip from my mouth, and when they landed, they were no big deal at all. Each time we were together, we slipped into our own existence. The world blurred around us. Him walking his bike beside me, both our bags slung over our shoulders, on opposite sides, so as not to get in between us. Every little thing held meaning for us.

Every day after work, Brian would buy a newspaper at the corner store closest to my bus stop. Daily, he pretended to be engrossed in the articles, secretly waiting for my arrival. He would just happen to see me waiting and make his way over to me. At the end of the day, I couldn't wait to see him. (He confessed after we were married that he had a very heavy, full bag each week of mostly unopened, unread newspapers.)

Brian wanted to talk more with me. So far, we had only seen one another during the work week, and only if either one of us met outside. He asked for my phone number twice, and I refused. I was waiting for my divorce to be complete. Oh, how I wanted to give him my number! It took a lot of self-control not to. I wanted to talk to him, but I had made a commitment to God, as well as my future ex-husband, and until my divorce was official, I would not date or jeopardize my integrity. As yet, I had not explained this to him and feared I may soon lose my chance to have a future with him. His co-workers told him to forget me and move on, taunting him with my rejection. He would not move on. He didn't feel he was being rejected. He built up his courage to ask me a third time. He must have been thinking about it for our entire conversation while I waited at my bus stop, because it wasn't until I was on the first step, boarding my bus that he finally asked me again, and once again, I said no. I felt that familiar tug at my heart, warning me not to push this guy away. The driver was annoyed, the door was closing. I quickly added that we could email, and shouted out my address. As we pulled away, I saw him scratch it down on one of his invoices for work.

I raced to my computer the moment I got home to check my email. And I waited. My next-door neighbor was such a great sport. Whenever I was about to "talk" to him, I'd call her over to be my chaperone. Often, I didn't get much done at home; I'd wander in close proximity to my computer, in case I missed a message. Things were great!

Sometimes, the things he would say sounded too good to be true. Was he just trying to impress me? I was already impressed. If he was lying to me, then I would be crushed. Brian was not one to try to impress. I would learn that soon enough. He was who he was. Take it or leave it. He had nothing to prove to anyone. He was by far the most confident person I would ever meet. He spoke of how he was asked to teach English to children in one of the countries he visited while travelling around the world. He had worked hard and saved his money. Then, he humbly packed up a few things, including his bike, got on a plane, and travelled, but not as a tourist. He wanted to experience life like the locals. He lived simply. He saved to be able to do what he enjoyed. Running, cycling, travelling, flying, photography...he had many talents and interests.

Our patient courtship continued. Brian would walk me to my elevator at work and say goodbye, only to see me again 20 minutes later as I made my way to the building's basement, collecting the firm's mail. He found ways to meet me while I did all my bank deposits and knew my exact schedule for the morning and afternoon runs. He'd escort me to the courthouse and back again. Together, we knew the homeless on each of their "spots", so that when I would enter one bank, they would holler at Brian, "She's in the bank, Brian!" Or smirk at me when they knew I would be going where he had just entered. Brian would squeal his bicycle brakes, announcing he was coming up behind me. I would leave him little notes in his tires or handlebars (once I was free to date again), with our homeless friends standing guard to make sure he got them.

Sometime before my divorce was final, I asked my bishop if it would be okay if Brian came to a drop-in volleyball game being held at a local school by some church members. As long as we didn't arrive together or leave together and we weren't alone, it would be fine. I did not want to mess this up! I arrived extra early, just in case he was there, so I could see him. The game began. I kept looking at the clock. He was so late. I kept playing. No Brian. I played my personal best; who knew when he would show up? I had to look great! Still no Brian. Where was he? Was he standing me up? He didn't seem the type. A glance at the clock confirmed there was so little time left. Maybe he had stood me up. Suddenly, a tall, thin guy entered the room. He had on a pair of light-rimmed glasses and unruly, curly, brown hair. Was this Brian? (I had not seen him with his helmet off as yet, and he was wearing glasses I hadn't seen on him before.) He looked different in shorts, without his helmet and shoulder bag.

He took a seat on the school bench along the gym wall. We were in the middle of a rally, so I had to pay attention. (I couldn't look foolish, now could I?) When there was a break, I looked down at the shoes he had just put on...he was wearing girls' sneakers with twice the amount of necessary laces: one hot pink, the other lemon yellow. Each tied bow was large and ridiculous. Was this a joke? He showed up late and put his showy shoes on to play volleyball with me? This was our first unofficial non-date.

Seemingly oblivious to these Rainbow Brite shoes, he simply smiled at me and made his way over to the opposite court. Thankfully, the game resumed, the volume in the room increased, and the pounding in my chest could not be heard. Who was this mysterious man?

He confessed afterwards how he only had clip-in cycling shoes to wear, no runners at the time. His tardiness was due to him frantically calling everyone he knew to borrow some sneakers. In the end, all he could rummage up were his roommates' girlfriend's outdated shoes. He absolutely wasn't about to miss the opportunity to be with me. He was so brave to show up like that, instead of stand me up. I gained so much respect for him.

Sometime during the game, we entered into our own existence again. Surrounded by people, we were the only two in the entire room. I have no idea how the rest of the game went. It was as if I had been given permission to just *be* in this moment. Time moved slowly. Anyone else's opinion did not matter to me. We bashfully smiled at each other, and giggled if we messed up a play. If I were standing on a red line, he would stand on the same red line, so that both of our feet were facing, making a connection. Energy seemed to escape his being, rushing to collide with mine. We both yearned to be connected in every possible way. It was new. It was exciting. It was fabulous.

I would soon grow to love every bit of Brian. He became my Brye Guy and I became his Nettie. (A name I cherish from only him). He went out of his way for me every opportunity he had. If he was leading the way in his car, he didn't speed. If our cars got interrupted by a light or another car, he would simply pull over to the side of the road, turn on his hazard lights, and wait until all cars passed. Then, when I got close to him, he would merge, and we would begin again; never losing sight of the other. He was always considerate, putting my needs before his own, and I went from being surprised to being so appreciative.

Here's a simple example: if he had a chocolate bar, he'd unwrap it and ask if I would like some, before he even took a bite. This meant a lot to me. He didn't dive in selfishly, nor wait to give me the last bite. In fact, he not only offered the first bite, he'd ask again, and even give up the last, if he thought it would simply make me smile. He opened every door for me, not out of duty, but because he valued me, and I could always feel it. He was my king, and I was his queen.

As with anything in life, when things start to get better, along comes a bump in the road. What seemed like hours away from divorce, my very-soon-to-be-ex-husband unexpectedly arrived at my house. Earlier that week, he had sent roses to my work, and now, out of the blue, said he wanted to work things out. I hadn't seen or heard from him in months. My little girl would wait on the door step for their scheduled time together... and he wouldn't show. I had to pick up the pieces of her broken heart. Up until I had met Brian, I had been trying to make our marriage work— for almost a year! Now here I was ...I had finally found someone who I was so deeply connected to, someone who was loving me for who I really was, not who they thought I was or wanted me to be. Someone who, unlike my ex-husband, wanted to be with me. I was moving on with my life.

David and I had been talking in the entranceway of my small townhouse. He said he missed me and suggested we could try again. He did look sweet and apologetic, yet he seemed like a stranger to me. Even though my compassionate female instincts felt badly he was hurting, there was a disconnect. Less than two months remained before the divorce was final. Prior to Brian, I had spent numerous hours on my knees, pleading with Heavenly Father to change David's heart and make our marriage work. Here was an answer to my prayer, but I no longer wanted it. Too much had happened; too much time had passed. Standing just inside the screen door, and without warning, he leaned in and kissed me. I was in shock and didn't know what to do. I just stood there, hands at my side, eyes wide open, not returning the brief kiss. We spoke a few awkward words, he left, and I shut the main door. What had just happened? There was no love in that kiss. I would not go back to a man who left me for another woman. I had been shown I had value, and this would never work with David.

Within moments, my doorbell rang. Expecting it to be David either pleading or retracting his case, I was surprised to see Brian! His face looked so betrayed. He had seen the whole thing, and my heart broke. I explained to him what had happened in all honesty, with nothing to hide. Inside, the Spirit spoke very loud and clear: "If you let him leave, he will never come back." I knew I could not lose him. I knew I loved him.

Are You Ready for a Miracle?

1). How do you expect good things to come to you?

a). I don't.

b). I wait for life to be good to me, because I deserve it.

c). I try to be my best self to attract the best people and events in my life.

2). How can you be your best self?

a). I read copious self-help books, but do not apply anything. The books are good reads, though.

b). I go to therapy just to talk, and talk, and talk, without taking any initiative to put into practice the therapy part of the session.

c). I practice saying positive truths about *me,* my truest best friend, combined with therapy, good books, and good people.

3). How can you trust your feelings?

a). I don't believe you can do anything based on how you feel, not even love. It has to be logical.

b). I'm usually confused about my feelings. I don't trust them, because I haven't figured out how.

c). When my heart is warm, or I get goosebumps, if the feelings I have feel good, then I trust them. If I feel uneasy or sick, I know to stay away.

TIPS

1). **A first impression doesn't have to be the final impression!**

This one seems almost silly to write, yet I feel it is important, nonetheless. We often feel the anxiety of making that first impression. Here's a quote to you from me, and I'm pretty sure I am not quoting someone else here, "You don't have to be perfect to be great!" I am here to tell you that if it's meant to be, it will be. Yes, Brian was not showing his best self the first day I laid eyes on him, but my heart had been moved in ways I wasn't expecting. If you mess things up the first time, whether it be in a meeting or on a date, take a deep breath. You don't know if their hearts were moved in your favour, and if they weren't, then next. No worries. There is a bigger plan. Trust in the plan.

2). **The importance of keeping promises.**

Before I get started on this one, let me preface this by saying, sometimes life happens, and you aren't able to make that date or deadline. What I am talking about here are sacred covenants or promises. Promises you make to God, your spouse, and your family. Binding contracts. Legal contracts. Be true to your word. Be a person of integrity. Value your value. Show your inner strength, your strength of character. If you have slipped up and made a mistake, own up to it and make it right. No one is perfect, but stop making excuses. People not only respect you when you are integrous, but you will also respect yourself.

3). **All choices have consequences.**

Like I've always taught my children, you have the freedom to make your own choices in life, but you can't control the consequences. In that moment when David returned to my doorstep, the universe presented me with two options. Each had consequences: returning to a loveless marriage where great trust was broken or tell the truth to Brian and start a relationship built on love and trust.

Remember, even our thoughts have consequences. If in my thoughts I had chosen to be deceitful and hide what had happened from Brian, he would have left that night, and not returned, and our story would be entirely different.

4). **Clothes don't make the person.**

Nor does the *stuff*. Be yourself. You make the person. Brian wore those ridiculous sneakers with dignity. Have dignity. The Merriam-Webster Dictionary says dignity is "the quality or state of being worthy, honored, or esteemed". When you are comfortable being you, people are comfortable with you.

Selflessness is also a wonderful personality trait. Find who you really are inside and give of yourself, even if it is simply opening the door for someone, or sharing a chocolate bar with a loved one!

5). **Tell the truth.**

Telling the truth builds trust. Saying even the scariest truths can build trust in relationships. Be mindful here. Telling your loved one that their new haircut looks stupid is not the kind of truth I am talking about.

Almost immediately after Brian and I were married, we sat together talking. A thought popped into my head: *What would I do if David were to come again and want me back?* I felt that if I let this thought continue to grow, it would become a problem in our marriage. Do I tell him this or keep it to myself? I decided to be honest...always. As I mentioned this to Brian, the thought released from me. My spirit sighed. Funny how this thought never returned to haunt me once it was released.

Chapter 3

The Dates

I was so excited. I checked with the lawyers at work to confirm my divorce was final before I got the divorce paper in my hand. Yes. The judge had signed my dissolution of marriage. David had time to contest, and he did not. I got this fabulous news on April first. This was no April Fool's Day prank. This was real. I was liberated. The wait was over. I could finally go on a date with Brian.

A new temple was being erected in Alberta. A place where couples and families could be sealed together for time and all eternity. Brian and I met at the temple construction site that evening. We talked and laughed and danced in the parking lot. I don't even remember if we had any music playing! Again, we were in our own world. Our "Lala Land". We were limited on how close we could get to the temple, what with all the construction site fencing. I felt such peace and love as I had not as yet experienced before. We leaned in and shared our first sweet little kiss. I wondered how silly this was to share our first kiss on April Fool's Day. Was it a good or bad sign of what was to come? But the temple was a fabulous sign of an eternal existence with this man.

Shortly after, Brian made plans to take me out for dinner, followed by dancing at a church dance. He came in and patiently waited while I finished doing my hair in the powder room. My ex- husband worked in a kitchen cabinet warehouse, and had left a heavy mirrored cabinet door behind. I had no other portable mirror, so I was using it to check the back of my hair. That thing was massive and difficult to lift, yet I seriously had nothing else. Lifting it up was a full arm workout. As I went to place it down, it slipped from my nervous, sweaty hands and slammed onto the top of my foot. I hollered in pain, and Brian came rushing to my aid. Oh, did it hurt. I was embarrassed and super-disappointed that I had ruined our date, but Brian was not discouraged. We both desperately wanted to go. He helped me hobble to his car.

We ate at an elegant restaurant downtown. I wish I knew which one, but I was so smitten I don't remember, and I have no idea what we ate. We spoke about everything and anything. The conversation was fluid and natural. I remember feeling again as though we were in our own bubble. Everything just outside our table was gone, and no one else existed. We connected in some cosmic way. Our souls had become reunited. We had finally found each other again. Outside of our table was literally a blur. The server barely came to check on us. (Or did they...?) Before we knew it, several hours had gone by, and it was getting late, very late. My foot was still a bit swollen, so Brian, seizing the occasion to wrap his arms around me (and hearing no complaints from me), placed me on his back and carried me to the car. We drove to the church, because we didn't want this night to be over, but the dance was just finishing, and I was in no condition to dance anyhow. We sat in the car and talked and talked. There was magic between us.

Laying on the floor in my bedroom, with my phone tucked under my chin, I listened to Brian's soothing voice as he not only spoke, but sang to me. The first song he ever sang was "You are My Sunshine"! Sure, he had a melodic voice, but he messed up all the words. Laughing, he tried again, and I joined him to help him out. He wasn't one to remember lyrics. He mostly didn't listen to the words of any song. He simply loved the music. Sometimes, I would have to inform him of what the inappropriate song was saying. He'd then be a little sad, because the music was so catchy and just put something else on. However, the range of music Brian enjoyed was incredible. Radiohead, opera, the simple sweet sound of an instrument (he especially enjoyed the sound of a piano), and the Buena Vista Social Club. However, U2 was by far his favourite, and he actually knew all the words to their songs! (He had one cassette tape he took with him while he cycled the world. U2's Joshua Tree. And when it broke from overuse, he took apart the cassette, taped it back together, then wound it all back up. He was a patient man alright.) "Ave Maria" was his favourite Christmas song, but he liked to especially sing the phrase *I'm dreaming of a white Christmas* over and over in the summer to tease us, because he also loved to be outside in the snow.

It was during a phone call that he first said, "I love you." It felt so right, like a missing puzzle piece, everything aligned. My head marveled at what all this could mean. My heart knew. My inner me knew. This was right. Heaven was bringing us together.

Silly, cheesy things became our norm. (Laughing, we'd say that we sure loved "cheese".) We sat together on the cement slab that was meant to resemble a backyard in the condo where I lived, and wrote with chalk every possible love message to each other, until the pad was filled to its entirety. "I love you," "You are my love," "You are my best friend," "I'll love you forever," could never be removed from us, even when the rains fell, washing the words away.

(Love notes on the back yard cement pad, Alberta)

Being on a tight, single mom budget, I would sometimes park my car in a far-off lot downtown, where it was free. Every day after work, Brian would hop off his bike and walk me to my car, carrying any bags or packages I had, while balancing his bike with one hand. If he could manage, he'd throw my bag over his shoulder and take my hand in his free one. This time, however, he wasn't accompanying me to my car. I had to hurry and couldn't waste time, as I had to race off and pick up my little girl from daycare. As I approached my car, I saw an enormous bouquet of flowers from the very posh, artsy florist shop downtown, cha-ching! (Brian was a very frugal man, except when it came to showing me he loved me.) Under my wiper was a card. I looked all around and could see no one. As I opened the card, I heard the familiar squealing of his bike brakes and looked up. He had hurried on ahead, placed the large bouquet of flowers and card on my windscreen and hid around the corner to watch my reaction. When he sneakily approached, I ran and threw my arms around him and giggled with delight. I appreciated everything this amazing man did for me.

On many mornings, we would sit together downtown and enjoy his favourite muffin together, a Morning Glory, before his buzzing radio would interrupt us, announcing his next delivery trip. Once, a sweet lady he worked with snapped a picture of us, remarking that one day we would want to remember this. How right she was. I am grateful for her picture.

(Brian and Annette dating downtown. Photographer unknown.)

Talking all night was not figurative. We literally spoke from after my little girl went to sleep until the morning alarm went off and I headed off to work. This lasted for days on end. We never ran out of things to talk about. We loved sharing and learning more about the other. If the line went quiet, I worried I had said something wrong or he was bored. Sometimes, I thought he had fallen asleep. "Brian?" "Yeah? I'm just listening to you." Before I could doubt him, he would ask a question about what I had been talking about. He just did that. He'd listen intently, take a moment to think about and digest what was said, and then respond intellectually. I loved him all the more for being so pensive. The morning sun would break, I'd gather the phone, and leave it on the bathroom counter. We'd both rush through our showers and race back to the phone. "Are you still there?" We'd place the phone on speaker and get ready for our day "together". When the clock announced I had to leave for work, we'd both say goodbye a hundred times, then wait for the other to hang up, then laugh because neither one could. Then, on the count of three, we'd hang up at the same time. Even that didn't always work, and we'd repeat the goodbye process again. This was not just a dating thing. It never ended, (as some people's love affairs do once they get married). For all the years we were married, we could never say goodbye. It hurt too much.

After many sleepless nights (I was so high on love that I seemed to manage better than I should have), a co-worker told me I looked terrible. I never felt happier in my entire life! I had a friend— a best friend— who had so much to say, but who also listened with real intent to everything I said. He was the only person in my life who had ever shown so much interest in me. I felt I had worth when I was with him. I knew he loved me, and that was such a remarkable feeling.

And then there were the dreams. I'd dream about him throughout the night and wake up with a smile on my face. He admitted months later how he would dream about me, too. We both had these moments where we couldn't help but smile while walking alone, these big foolish grins, and I admit, sometimes a giggle would slip out. People would look at us curiously or avoid us all together.

One evening when he was leaving my place, I felt my first of many intense feelings for Brian. He felt it, too. Love suddenly was not a strong enough word. We could find no word that worked for this immense, strong connection that we had for one another. As he reluctantly left, I waved my hand in sign language for I love you. Since that moment, that has become our family's special *thing*. When kids would sing in concerts, or be walking away to school, our hearts connected with the hand symbol *I love you*.

I asked him if he wanted to know more about the church. He did. He met with the missionaries on his own. I never had any part of his conversion in that regard. If he had questions, he asked the missionaries. I had been praying about Brian, wondering if it was right to marry him. He talked of being together into the distant future with me each time we spoke. One day, he showed up at my place and said a date. I immediately thought this was the day he wanted to marry me and got scared— I wasn't ready for that yet. It was the day he decided to get baptized. Which meant if we did get married, we could be sealed as husband and wife in the temple for all eternity, not just until death do us part.

As Brian was finishing flight school and needed the hours, he would take me flying with him. On this particular day, as we flew above the homes, the fields, and the farmland, I sensed a change sweep over him. In that instant, I knew he was about to ask me to marry him. I still wasn't sure I was ready. My heart had been broken when I was married before, and I was scared. Plus, it was pretty early, according to the world. It had only been a couple months, if that! So, like any other time in my life, I prayed. I prayed so earnestly that he would *not* ask me to marry him up here, so very high up above everything. I was worried. What if I offended him by saying no and we crashed! As soon as I said 'amen' in my head, the feeling shifted back. (When we got married, I asked him if I was right about that day and the possible proposal, and he said yes!) God was always in the details.

Dating

1). If you were to write a resume about yourself in order to be considered for a date, what would you write?

   a). I would *upgrade* myself by stretching the truth about a lot of things. I am boring. Who would want to get to know me? Afterwards, I might clear things up once we've been dating.

   b). I would list all my accomplishments when I was younger, because I don't have much in the way of accomplishments now.

   c). If I have trouble seeing the good in myself, I would ask my loved ones for help.

2). How do you stay vulnerable and safe?

   a). I hardly think about consequences, and I often get hurt.

b). I hardly ever give my whole self to anyone. What if they don't love me for me?

c). I stay close to my faith, believing that I am enough as I am, and that trials are a part of life.

3). What do you do if someone feels you have lied, or you've been caught in a lie?

a). I wait until I get caught and keep lying to cover it up.

b). I defend myself.

c). I tell the truth. I humble myself, apologize, do my best to make things right and hope for the best.

TIPS

1). **The beginning isn't the end.**

Why do we so often look back at the newness, the beginning of our dating relationship with a tinge of sorrow? It is a new and exciting time of revelation and connection, sure. Let's think about springtime. Here in Alberta, where it can be extremely cold (an average winter temperature is -30'C, not to mention the wind chill!) and the ground is covered with snow for what seems like at least eight months out of the year, springtime is a very exciting time for me. Since I love flowers, I tend to search out the earliest signs of buds in our yard. This can be compared to the beginning of your relationship. Why stop there? Can you not be as equally excited about the flowers as they begin to open? And then as time goes by, and the flower petals fall, can we not also be happy to hold on to our loved one's hand as the leaves turn into majestic reds and oranges?

We can put in some effort, even a little more effort, like we did when we first met, add some compost to the soil, and see what blossoms.

2). **Love is not lust.**

Yup. I said it. Love is built on friendship and trust. Lust and love evoke such intense emotions. Have you ever rushed into intimacy only to find it was short-lived, not reciprocated, or left you feeling guilty inside? I can speak for myself here: love is more powerful and enduring than lust. Love lasts forever.

3). **Let it be organic.**

Trust the plan. Forcing makes things break. I have found throughout my life that when things are forced, they fall apart. Brian and I worked so well because a lot of it just... happened. I am not saying we didn't do anything to make it happen, we did. The difference is, I wasn't calling him without him calling me back. In fact, I let him call me first. (heehee) I wasn't chasing him down, I let him do the chasing (heehee), and when he did, I reciprocated. I let him know how awesome he made me feel when he did things I liked. Because he truly loved me, he would do those things that made me happy again and again, just to see me smile. The same happened in reverse. He appreciated me, and I lived to see him smile. It was organic.

4). **Give it away.**

Have you ever noticed how whenever you give of your time, your talents, or your stuff, you get so much more in return? The opposite is also true. When we greedily hold on to our time, talents, and stuff, we seem to keep losing in the end. Give it away. Give away your time with your loved one. Get off the phone. Stop playing mindless games on your device, and look up! Give away your talents by not only giving the absolutely needed hugs, but service. How hard is it when you hear your spouse heading to the shower to grab them a clean towel? Betcha it makes them feel so loved by your sacrifice. Give away the compliments. How often do you see something wonderful they do, but you keep it to yourself? Why not tell them? The more you notice, the more you'll continue to notice, and the more you verbalize this to them, the more they will want to rise to the occasion.

5). **Game on!**

Brian and I liked to make life fun. Be creative in your marriage and in your family life. Let's briefly talk about how to make a game out of life with your spouse. Here are some personal examples (please be mindful of your partner's own love language). When we were washing dishes, I'd blow bubbles off my hand into his face. Then, the kids and I would run like crazy before he tickled us. Folding laundry became a rolled-up sock fight. Board games as a couple would sometimes turn into a game of how many kisses were owed to the other, or who got to change the next diaper (depending on the stage we were in). When the kids were little and didn't understand the concept of eating with utensils, we "punished" them by having a no utensils, no hands supper!

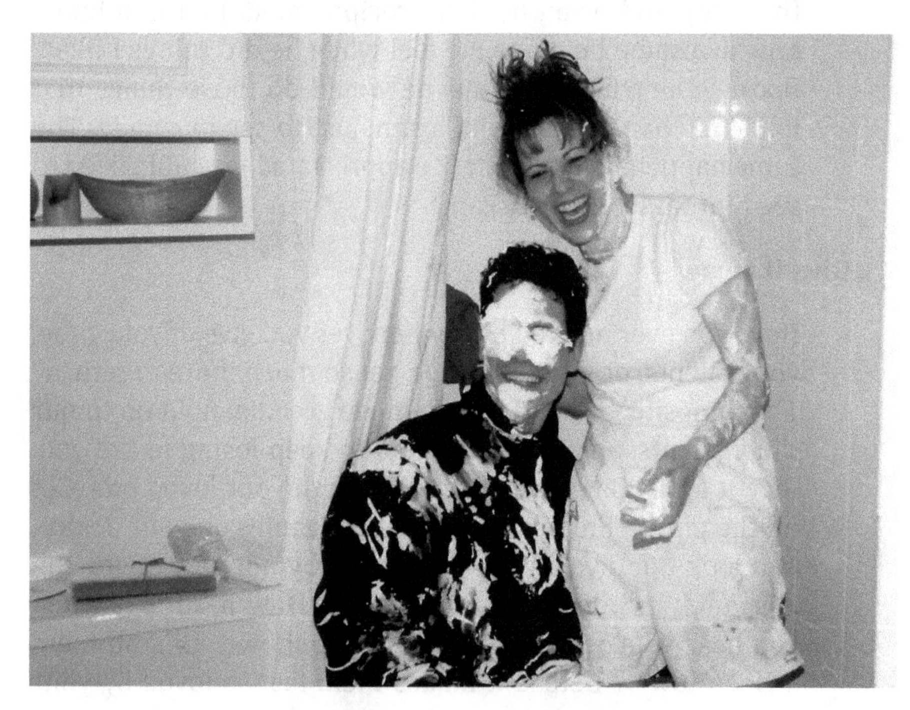

(Brian and Annette and the shaving cream fight! Picture taken by unknown)

Chapter 4

The Magic

Brian showed up at my house early in the morning. My instincts said today was the day he would ask me to marry him. He had been talking about our future since the second day we met! From the early morning until late evening, we walked and talked and walked and talked. Around downtown, we'd sneak into alley ways for a tender kiss. We continued into the river valley, but then drove over toward the zoo! We had breakfast at a quaint little restaurant and picnic in the park for a late lunch (that he had packed very early that morning). To be honest, by the time it was late afternoon, I was beginning to doubt my judgement and thought he would never ask me. He returned our picnic items to his little red Honda Civic hatchback, circa 1990, and we went walking again. We made our way to some old wooden stairs climbing up the side of the hill in the river valley. Turning to look out over the blue sky, we sat down for a rest. Brian kneeled down in front of me, and took out a tiny little box. When he opened the box and took out the ring, he dropped it into the crack of the stairs! Luckily, he was able to retrieve the ring with his long, thin fingers. And then, I heard the sound of fireworks, and so did he! But it was not a holiday, nor was it even dark outside - it was late afternoon! But we heard them, and joked that the heavens and our future kids were so happy we were together. I believe now that we were right. The heavens were rejoicing.

(Engagement photo by Joanne Domier MacLennan)

(Engagement photo by Joanne Domier MacLennan)

He was gentle, articulate, humble, artistic, well-travelled, well-read, honest, sweet, intelligent...he was my miracle, and I told him so. In a life of heartache and disappointment, he was my everything, and I literally called him *My Miracle.* I was finally happy and so very much so. My life seemed like a fairytale. We shared all our thoughts and feelings. We had no secrets. We made the mistake of asking family when they could come to our wedding. Since no one could agree (and some thought we were crazy and didn't want to come), we decided one day to get married right away. (Let me explain something here; I prayed so earnestly and so often and got a confirmation that marrying Brian was, indeed, the right thing. It worked in his favour that he met the criteria on my prayer list, too!) We were married two weeks after we made that decision. I had fabulous friends, like Marni, who planned all the decorations, Holly and others, who took care of the food, Leslie, who made not only my wedding dress from simply looking at a picture in a magazine, but my bridesmaid dresses, too—and in such a remarkably short time!

We married in July. Yes, five months after we met! He had family there, but I did not. No one. Not a single person from my family, except my beautiful daughter. Instead, I had some very supportive friends.

Our wedding day was like a scene in a movie. One of Brian's close friends, Dan, picked me up to escort me to the chapel. It was such a hot day in Edmonton; 33°C. Dan decided we need not be on time, but let the poor groom sweat it out a bit. Along the way, we spotted a sweet little girl on the corner with her lemonade stand. It was hot. He wasn't getting me there any faster, so I hopped out and walked over to her. Her mom ran out with camera in hand, and of course, my drink was free!

As my heart yearned to get there faster, Brian was feeling anxious, too. Our bishop decided to pull Brian into his office and there deliver the sad news that I was not coming. I had changed my mind! Brian's face went red, his stomach lurched, and his heart sank. The bishop was joking, but Brian did not find this at all amusing.

That day, I walked the aisle by myself. There he was, standing tall, looking handsome and oh so sweet waiting for me. We said our vows, he placed a beautiful ring upon my finger, and then turned and asked Amberly to come to him. He asked her to give him her ring finger, and he placed a tiny ring on her, symbolic of him being united to both of us.

Photos came next. Our chapel was within walking distance to the venue for our outdoor pictures. So, we did just that. Hand in hand, Brian and I made our way. I started to walk briskly, and he stopped me. He wanted to relish in this moment. Cars honked, and people shouted congratulations as they passed. It was magical.

The heat was incredible! Off came the pantyhose, and away we went to 7-11 for a slurpee! Dan wanted to take more pictures of us as we played in the park! Brian's pant legs rolled up as we walked in the sand. He pushed me on the swings. We were always loving life and in our own world.

(Brian and Annette on their wedding day. Picture taken by Joanne Domier MacLennan)

(Brian and Annette on their wedding day. Picture taken by Joanne Domier MacLennan)

(Slurpee time at 7-11 right after wedding photos were taken. It was such a hot day! Picture possibly taken by "Dan the Man")

(Playing at the park on their wedding day, taken by "Dan the Man")

(Amberly playing at the park with her mom and new dad on their wedding day, picture taken by "Dan the Man")

On our wedding night, we stayed at an old Victorian hotel. He already knew so much about me in such a short span of time. He carried me over the threshold, and before I knew it, he was just nonchalantly sitting on the bed. Waiting. I had so many bobby pins poking into my head that needed to be taken care of first. This was the moment of, *gulp*, being with him, and I really wanted to postpone it. I was scared. Why was I scared? I shouldn't have been. I had been married before. This wasn't my first time. But I was. I was almost terrified.

He must have been wondering why I was taking so long in the bathroom, and came to check on me. There we sat on the floor, beside the tub filled with water and rose petals. (He had Dan drive me around while he raced up and got the room ready.) One by one, he undid each and every pin curl until my now crazy hair was free.

Right from the start, we had no secrets. We shared one email, one bank account, we almost shared a Facebook account, and that also meant peeing in front of him! Anytime a friend of the opposite sex was involved in our lives, whether that was just in conversation or planning a get-together, we told the other all that was said. In fact, we did our very best at ensuring he did not go out with a woman one-on-one; I was present. The same was true with me. One day, I was asked to meet a director friend for lunch, and I insisted his wife come along, since Brian was out of town. We valued our relationship too much to let anyone or anything tamper with it. We took great care to keep this relationship healthy, trustworthy, and loving.

He had a way of making me face every fear when we were together, no matter how small it seemed. I was encouraged by simple words. When I decided to take on acting classes or tackle a writer's program, he'd lovingly say, "Nettie, you'd be great at that, because you are so..." smart, outgoing, funny, brave... the list of compliments was long.

(Brian with two of his girls, Amberly and Annette, taken by John Tilley)

Brian loved Amberly as his own little girl. They made necklaces, and imprinted hands in cement. We had David over and asked if Brian could adopt her. I only saw Brian cry twice. That night, he cried at how her dad could so easily give her up. He said how remarkable, smart, and beautiful she was, and it broke his heart. Before we knew it, we were in the courtroom, where she became a Tilley, like us. After we were married, having had a baby girl, we were sealed as a family for time and all eternity in the same temple where Brian and I had shared our first kiss. He and I – married and sealed to our children for forever. What a great blessing. It wasn't until later that I truly valued this great blessing. We were to be married not just for this life, but for forever. We would be with our children, not for this life, but for forever. I thought I cherished Brian then, but as time goes by, I cherish him even more. And being a forever family is the most priceless gift.

(Edmonton, Alberta Temple of the Church of Jesus Christ of Latter-Day Saints, taken by Annette Tidball)

There was a time when I was married to David that I truly thought I would never be able to have more children. I wanted more. He did not. We tried and failed. Now I was with two little girls, one seven and the other a sweet baby. I wasn't being cursed. In fact, I went on to have two more little girls after that. I jokingly suggest that my last three were waiting for Brian to be their daddy.

I invited Brian inside my most inner circle of love and trust, my inner circle of safety and protection, where no one else had ever been before. My personal heart-wall that protected me from the harm and destruction from the outer world. I welcomed him in, and that's where he stayed. And why? Because he put my needs first. He loved me like the Savior. He was selfless and always in-tune with how my heart felt; how to treat me based on my heart's needs. We were connected, so that my heart was his heart.

(Brian with his girls. Paige, Maile, Savannah and Amberly taken by Annette Tilley)

(Brian and Annette -always holding on as tight as they could - picture by John Tilley)

Do You Believe in Magic?

1). If you've been hurt by loving someone, how do you love again?

a). I don't, and I judge everyone else who does. I shut down my heart and build a heart-wall for protection.

b). I pretend I'm in love to make the other person happy.

c). Not everyone will hurt me. I take the chance and have faith. I listen to any internal warning signs.

2). What's holding you back from creating magic with your spouse?

a). I don't like how others may judge me as different or odd.

b). I already pretend to the world through social media that we have magic; isn't that enough?

c). I love to see them smile. I lift them up as I continue to lift myself.

3). What keeps you from having an unjealous love?

a). I am insecure. I fear if I allow myself to love someone else's child or allow them to love their deceased loved one, or even if I have a love for my stepchildren's other parent, I will somehow be loved less.

b). I try to love without jealousy, I am just not there yet. I don't know how.

c). I have imperfect moments, but I am working on it. I simply tell myself it's okay to love. It's also okay to love from a distance if the circumstances are unfavourable.

TIPS

1). **Keep dating your spouse!**

Why wouldn't you want to? If you're married, then make it work. Friday nights were and are date night. It's established in our home, and our kids know that Friday is *date nigh*t. Let me say that again, Friday *is* date night. (You can pick your own night of the week, but you must sacrifice time each week to spend time together.) Who cares if you have no money to do anything?! That's when you get creative. Maybe you send kids to grandma's or you wait until they are in bed, or you arrange to see each other over a lunch break. Maybe you make a milkshake together, play cards, go for a walk holding hands, grab the kids' skateboard and learn something new, head to the library, do yoga at home, play tennis...whatever it is, change it up, and make it stick. I have often jokingly (but not joking) told the kids, if you don't date your spouse, what will you do if someone else comes along and gives them more attention than you are...? Invest in the love life of your marriage.

2). **Touch.**

We thrive on love. Touch can and *should* be used to uplift, encourage, and show love. Remember your first crush?

.nember when they accidentally brushed their hand .xt to yours? Find gentle ways to touch your spouse. At inner, sit next to them. Intertwine your legs or place your .oot on top of theirs. Hug! Hugs release happy feelings. Hug often. When my husband comes home, I like meeting him at the door, stepping onto the bottom stair (because I'm vertically blessed!), and reaching up to hug and kiss him. I see the smile on his face, and hugs make us feel happy. Such a simple thing to make the relationship grow. Find ways to appropriately touch the other during each day.

(Brian and Annette with the signature close embrace! Picture taken by Brian's Mummo, Aira Salomma in British Columbia)

3). **Be mindful.**

This is a saying we hear a lot these days. What do I mean by this? Our thoughts whirl about all day, and how often do we stop and listen? Better yet, do we stop and *correct* them? If we are watching our husband cut the grass and we find fault with it, the thought whirls in our head and we may not even notice it. Well, notice it! I have found when I am paying attention to these thoughts, I can correct them, and the sooner I do, the better I am for it. I want to be in control of what I think, not have my thoughts be the boss of me.

Instead of being frustrated, I have found if I actively think things like, *he has a good heart, he works hard for us, I know he is trying his best,* I begin to love him from the inside out. I begin to love his true self, from his heart outward. When I do that, my heart has a deeper connection to his.

4). **Take care of you.**

This may sound silly, but take a shower, wash your clothes, if you can- smell nice. I love the smell of a man. One day, I went in to the men's washroom to replace towels at the yoga studio. Everyone had left from the morning's session but... bam! As soon as I walked into that room, I could smell... a man! You know that smell of their bodywash or even (for goodness sake) their deodorant— it smelled good, and it lifted my mood and made me smile.

Exercise. Eat good foods. Stay healthy. Take care of yourself. Do it for yourself. Exercise lifts your mood. You can do this at home when you roll out of bed. It doesn't have to be expensive; just move your body more. Eat less sugar; sugar can affect how you feel. Be the great person you want to be.

5). **Love with an un-jealous love.**

When Brian came into our lives, he loved us from the inside out. This meant he was not jealous that I had been married before. He was not jealous that there was another man in Amberly's life, nor was he jealous that this man would/could be a part of our lives. Allowing your heart to open up to love others is a gift worth praying and working for.

Chapter 5

The Journey

Brian was so patient. Throughout our entire marriage, he would come with me wherever I was going and wait. I would follow him, too. Being together brought us so much joy, we didn't care what it was. If I were on set with a small acting part, he would come and quietly watch. If I was taking a musical theatre class, there he would be, waiting to drive me home (even though I could have driven home on my own), not stressed about how much time it took me to collect my things and say goodbye to everyone.

I never ever had to ask for help around the house. In fact, I used to lovingly tease him that he had OCD - Over Cleaning Disorder. He was quick to change diapers, (and we did cloth, clean 'em, at-home diapers!), vacuum the floor, mop, put clothes away, tidy the shoes in the front hall closet, wash windows, take out the garbage, rub little finger prints off the walls, all the while never complaining about helping. I'd ask him why he helped me so much, to which he answered: "I love you, Nettie. You have the hardest job, taking care of these precious little girls. I don't mind helping."

The longer we were married, the more patient he became, if that's even possible.

He frequently told me, "I love you Nettie, and I *like* to serve you." Then, he'd smile or grab me in a bear hug. When we were watching a movie together, and I would get up to go make a tea, he would jump up and say, "I can do that for you." I feel I treated him the same, with simple, meaningful acts of service, then returning and wrapping my arms around his shoulders or pressing my head into his neck. Serving one another was a special treat to show how much we loved the other. I had never been treated this way in my entire life. I have said that my previously damaged heart had numerous holes and let all love leak out, but because of Brian, my heart was repairing itself, filling and finding its purpose.

Once, he drove up north without us, (we hardly spent any time apart if we could help it), stopping at every place possible, looking for a flying job. He couldn't wait any longer to see us again. When it came time to come home, he didn't stop to rest (he knew better), but he drove for 24 hours! When he came to give me a big bear hug, his eyes were the most bloodshot eyes I had ever seen, and yet, because he had promised Amberly he would play at the park with her when he got home (believe me -she remembered and asked him), he said yes. Off we headed to the park, so he could play with her!

What set us apart from the everyday couples I see all around me? We kept the magic alive throughout our entire marriage. We both wanted to. Going for walks was a big thing for us. We loved being outside (and we had a very tight budget.) We were always touching. Our silent ways of letting the other know we loved them so much. Holding each other's hand, or holding hands with the kids. At church, the kids sat on either side of us, never in between, as we scooped our feet, interlocking our legs. Daily, we danced in the kitchen while cleaning. The kids would pretend to be grossed out and say *eww*, and comment that there was no music, to which Brye would respond, "There's music in our hearts," "It's the music of love," or "We are in La La Loveland, girls." We habitually engaged in flirtatious towel fighting, which typically ended with us chasing each other up the stairs, laughing and kissing one another after a tackle in the hallway. We'd stare at the other in awe at all the little things we appreciated about the other. "Wow, you are so great at paying attention to our daughter when she puts on her nonsensical plays, Brye! And then, you even ask questions!" Frequently writing love notes or letters and leaving these on the pillow, in a homemade lunch, or on my desk when we both worked downtown. We snuggled so closely that we even seriously considered buying a twin bed for just the two of us. To us, teasing to harm was not in our love vocabulary. Why tease to make the other feel sad or embarrassed? How did that ever help grow a relationship? We found that lifting the other lifted us individually and collectively as a family.

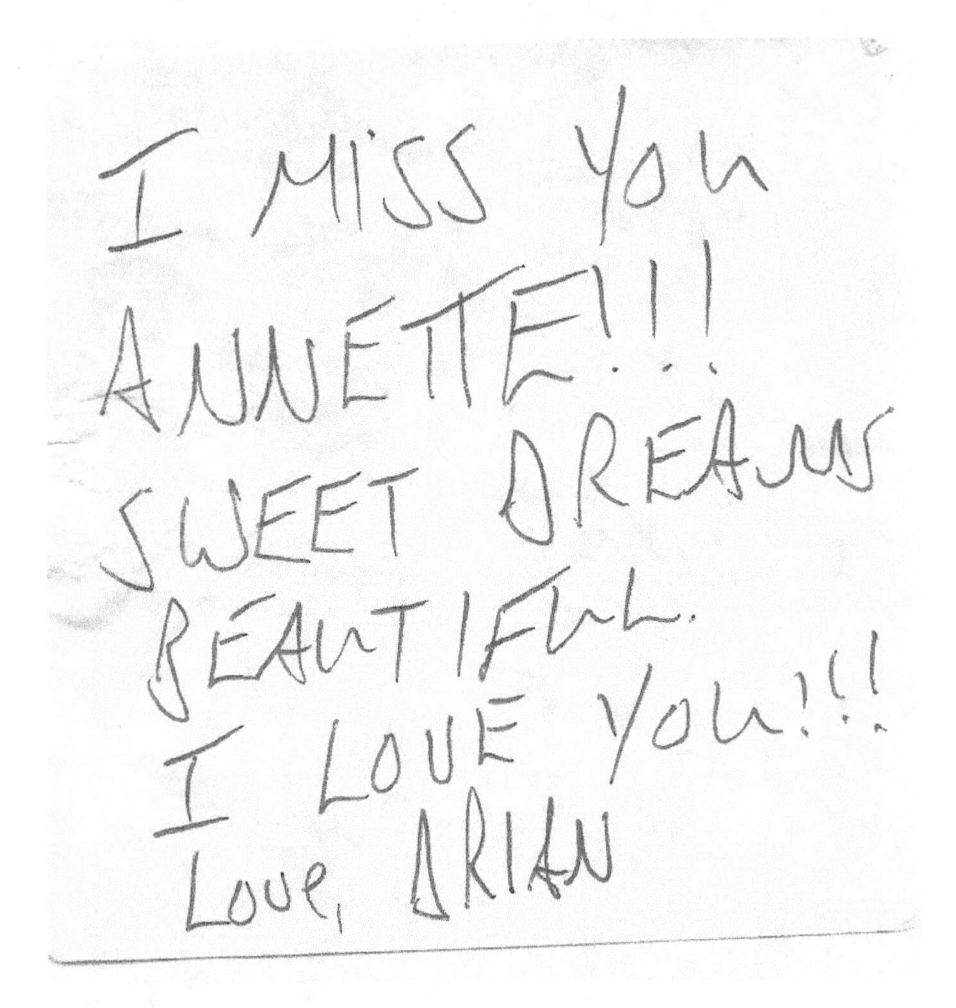

I MISS YOU
ANNETTE!!!
SWEET DREAMS
BEAUTIFUL.
I LOVE YOU!!!
Love, BRIAN

(One of the many love letters Brian wrote to Annette, just because)

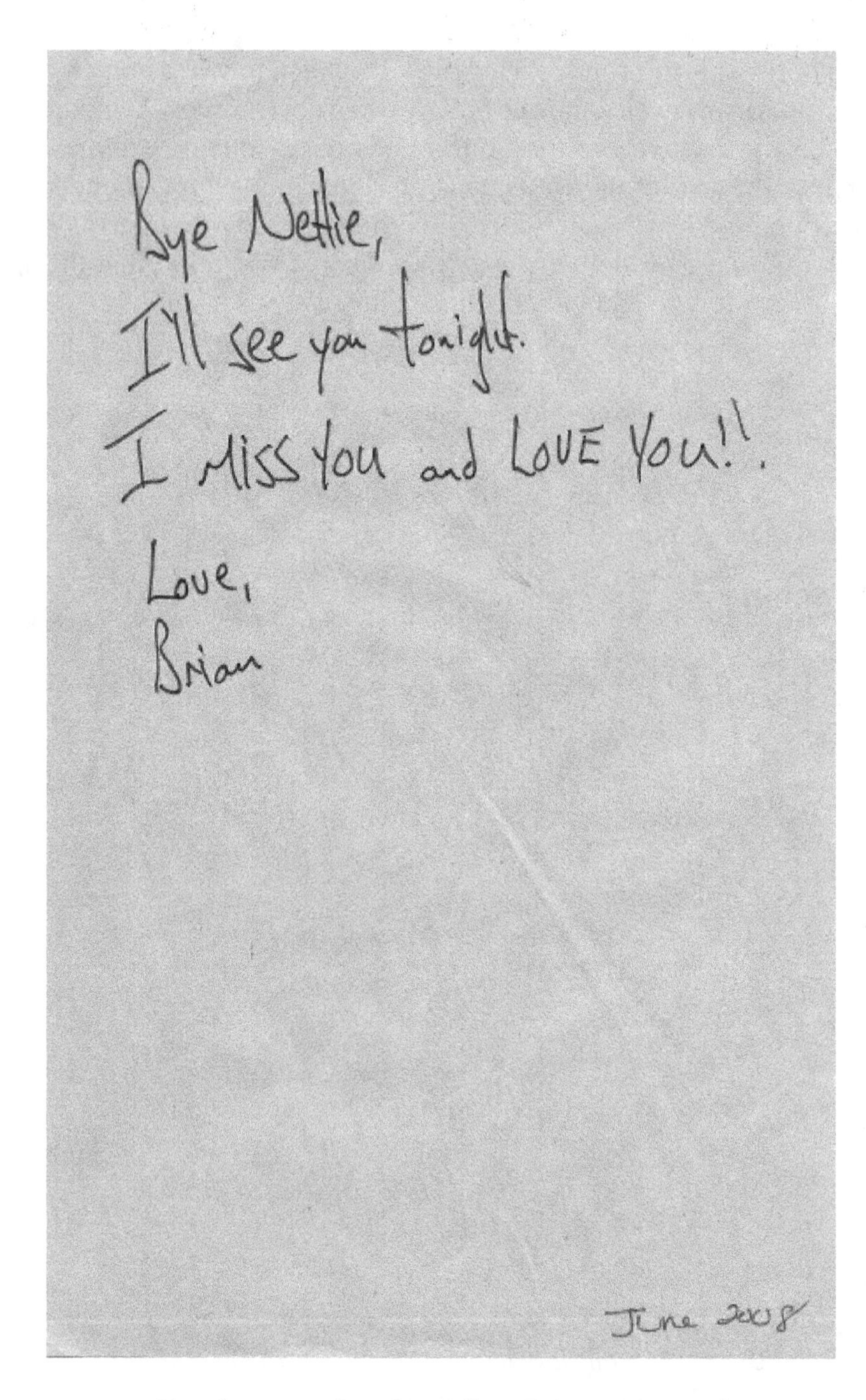
Bye Nettie,
I'll see you tonight.
I MISS YOU and LOVE YOU!!.
Love,
Brian
June 2008

(Another sweet love letter from Brian to Annette)

Brian would ask the girls, "Have you heard the news?" To which the girls would laugh and say, "Daddy, we already know the news! You love us!" Sometimes, they would say, "Daddy, you're crazy!" To which he always responded, "Crazy in love!" or "Crazy in love with your beautiful Momma!" and then reach out, kiss me, and turn to chase the screaming girls for kisses, too.

I just assume that every couple has their secret language or secret codes. The Hand Squeeze was one of ours; squeezing hands when it was time to go, time to pay attention, or I love you. We loved finding new terms of endearment, a.k.a. pet names. This was even more so when Brian heard on the radio that the more loving names you had for your spouse meant the greater the love you had for one another.

"You are *so* beautiful!" I can't even begin to tell you how many times, with awe and wonder, he would stop, look at me with new awareness, catch his breath, and say those words with such intensity that my heart leapt for joy. Probably more than 100 times a day. That man was so richly blessed with thoughtfulness. Even after the honeymoon stage, I would wake up to find Brian propped up on one arm, just watching me sleep. He had this look, like he had never seen me before or something. I have no idea how long he lay there, studying my face, as if he'd never see it again. I don't know how to explain it. He was mesmerized by my drooly face, my morning breath, and sleepy eyes. Each time, he would say in such a tender, touching way, from deep within his soul, that I was the most beautiful woman he had ever met. How was he so lucky to have me? And you know what? I began to believe him over time. I never felt more loved, more beautiful, more talented, more accepted for who I was, than with Brian. I was always beautiful to him. It never mattered what I was wearing; he looked at me with the same intensity. It was as though he saw me through a love lens. I could just be me, and he loved me. All of me. Even frizzy big morning hair and morning breath me!

We made a game out of life. I would try to finish brushing my teeth and spit before him, but I seemed to take too much time in the flossing department. This meant he would still spit and spray me and then chuckle. I'd frown and playfully whack at his shoulder.

One hot day, the girls and I were outside watering the flower beds and having a little water fight with cups and buckets. Grandpa John (Brian's dad) was over watching, laughing, and occasionally joining from the front porch step. Brian drove up and parked in front of the house. I aimed the hose at the passenger window. The girls laughed. Brian made a pretend "I'm gonna get you!" face at me and the girls, to which the little girls screamed and ran. Placing my thumb on the end of the hose, and hoping he wouldn't mind getting wet, I sprayed him down. He reached for me. The girls quickly joined in with little cups and buckets, missing him entirely. Grandpa was helping them to refill and run back. A full-on family water fight ensued. That's just how it was with him. He was always in a state of living a grateful life.

He always knew spending time— quality time— with loved ones was the most important thing in the world. We never had cable (we didn't want distractions from being a couple), and only once in a while would we even watch a VHS (yes, we were behind the times then), but we always had music on. Dancing with kids, watching our little girls show us their "moves", and singing. We played board games and card games at night when the kids were in bed, and we even turned simple games into a couples game where we would kiss and hold one another.

("I love you Brye Guy" in Alphaghetty noodles, taken by Brian Tilley)

We used food that had letters to spell "I love you," on the table. I'd leave him love notes under his pillow, in his pocket, in his work bag or pilot bag, anywhere. I couldn't tell him I loved him enough. He would do the same. He was very articulate, poetic and romantic. Even his penmanship had an artsiness to it. Here is what he said in a *just because* card:

> *"Dear Annette,*
>
> *When I kiss you, nothing else matters. When I'm with you, nothing else matters. With you, every petty thing becomes just that, petty. You, Annette, have a way of creating incredible sunshine and happiness in my life. Your mannerisms, way of talking and laughing, touch, support, love, and tenderness don't go unnoticed, baby. Annette, you're my dream come true. You're my one and only. I LOVE YOU!*
>
> *Love, Your husband forever, Brian."*

I kiss you
I paint love pictures
to you.
D.H. Lawrence

(Front of Artisan Love Card given to Annette from Brian, picture taken by Annette Tidball)

Dear Annette,

When I kiss you nothing else matters.
When I'm with you, nothing else matters.
With you, every petty thing becomes
just that, petty. You, Annette, have
a way of creating incredible
sunshine and happiness in my life.
Your mannerisms, way of talking and
laughing, touch, support, love and
tenderness don't go unnoticed, baby.
Annette, you're my dream come
true. You're my one and only.

I LOVE YOU!

Love,
Your husband forever Brian.

(Inside of card given to Annette, picture taken by Annette Tidball)

Sure, we had trials; love wasn't one of them. We held hands, and I'd still get tingles. I yearned to be with him and he with me. We didn't like being apart. Every year of our life together was like that. Some people feel this when they are dating, and, then, it dissipates—ours just grew stronger.

Besides the family tradition of using the sign for I love you, we also said, "I'll love you forever times infinity to the power of infinity." It just seemed like the most complete way to love. Never-ending, all-encompassing, forever love.

Special. Brian made everyone feel like they were special. When you spoke, he looked you in the eye and attentively listened, never interrupting. Somehow, he managed to stop what he was doing, no matter how important it was and still have time for you to feel special. Each girl believed they were his favourite, because they were. He informed the girls daily: "Mom is the best mom in the world and has the hardest job, so you look after her, okay girls?" He played Barbie dolls, and dressed up baby dolls. He got up in the night to care for the girls, because as he said, they were his children, too. One year, he sewed pajamas with me for their Christmas presents.

(Brian flying picture possibly taken by John Tilley)

When Brian was flying small aircraft doing pipeline patrol, he'd call ahead to let us know to run outside where he would tip his wings from side to side, waving at us. We never thought then how silly we must have looked to the world. Four girls and a mom waving and screaming up at the sky. But when he'd return home, we would all—including myself—run to the door in excitement and jump into his open arms.

Worry. I worried daily about losing him. I prayed with such intent throughout my day for his health and safety. I worried about him driving and flying and especially his heart. Brian's aortic valve in his heart was bicuspid where it should have been tricuspid. All I understood about this was three things: 1) His heart let blood back into the valve that should be there. 2) He had to eat well and stay fit to keep his heart strong. 3) One day, he may need a pig's heart valve to fix this. I'd lay my head on his chest and hear his super-strong, loud rhythm. My heart beat for him and his for me.

Anytime Brian was sitting down, I would come up behind him and wrap my arms around his neck. With each tender hug, kiss, or touch, love would gently escape my pores and collide with the reciprocal love he was sending me. It was truly tangible. At times when he would kiss me, I would open my eyes to watch him. His eyes were already staring at me, too. Memorizing the moment.

You must know by now that a relationship like this would not have been so magical if we had terrible thoughts about the other spinning around in our heads. Looking back, I can see how different my thoughts were with him, compared to my previous life. While taping a wall prepping it for paint, I would think how cute his bum was. He'd do tricks on his bike and my heart would flutter as I thought how sexy he was. He'd build a deck, a shed, or finish a basement with no prior knowledge, and I'd marvel at how intelligent he was. I was always thinking about how wonderful he was in some way. Put downs didn't cross my mind. And if my feelings got hurt, I was quick to forgive, although he was faster. This just made our relationship flourish. Our love grew stronger, and our hearts became knitted together in unity.

He was so comfortable being himself. I believe he wanted everyone to feel that way. It didn't matter what clothes you wore, and he certainly stuck to that rule. It's funny how it never truly bothered me. For instance, he liked to wear MEC fleece pants with an untucked blue dress shirt buttoned all the way to his neck. No neck tie. No matching pants, and he continued to wear unmatching socks. If it was winter, he would top this off with a large down jacket, large, clunky winter boots, and a funny-looking toque. (He wanted to buy a racoon-style hat, which I refused.)

He held numerous jobs. Interesting jobs. He was a bicycle courier and worked downtown when we met, and for some time after we were married. He also picked up dead bodies for a time and transported them from the place where they passed to designated funeral homes. He even drove around the province collecting money from payphones when they still existed.

In order to increase his flying hours, he flew skydivers. I remember sitting in the stands at a local baseball game when he *dropped* the skydivers into the baseball field. The girls and I were so proud. Often when he worked here, we would go up with his Dad to visit with the skydivers, eat lunch with Brian, and just watch. To switch things up a bit, the owner invited Brian to bring me up with him. Brye told me I had to put on a parachute *just in case.* I soon found myself sitting on the floor of the plane, beside Brian, but facing the back of the plane. He told me he was about to open the door to *drop* the divers, and that I should hold onto the bottom part of his seatbelt attached to his seat. A skydiver from the back was making his way toward me and shouted (the plane was very loud), would I mind sticking my leg out the open door, in order for them to have more room to jump. I agreed. No problem. The door opened, I felt the rush of the wind, but I had to be brave and stick out my leg. Oh my gosh! My leg snapped back so quick! I could feel my skin on the outer edge of the plane! I held onto Brian's seatbelt and peered over the edge. The jumpers were gone in a flash! My grip tightened, and my knuckles turned white. That's what he meant by just in case! Just in case I fell out of the plane!!

(Brian, Annette and baby Savannah at Eden North Parachute School picture taken by John Tilley)

(Brian did his second jump as a tandem, the first one was a solo elsewhere. Brian and Tim Douglas picture taken by John Smith at Eden Parachute School)

Pipeline patrol came next. His dad once asked me to take some pictures while I was up there with Brye. I agreed. Of course, Brian thought he was funny by turning the plane quickly each time I looked into the tiny hole of the older camera. I felt so sick. I can see his mischievous smile even now.

One day while flying, Brian noticed a big, burly grizzly bear knocking trees down as it ran. He knew up ahead was a man on a quad in the direct path of the approaching bear. He flew back to the animal, buzzing over it several times, until the bear changed direction. He may have saved that man's life that day.

In his flying career, he flew organs up north. He flew children who needed medical care from the north to the city. He chartered celebrities and people with a great deal of money to watch their horses race. Brian worked his way up to chief pilot at one of the companies. He made me proud. But every time he flew, and I had to force myself to go to sleep without him, I would place the phone under my pillow. That way, I could catch it immediately without waking the little girls when he called (and he always did), to say he had landed safely and was just putting the plane away in the hangar.

(Calm Brian... picture taken by unknown)

The economy was getting sticky, and he wanted to find work that was more secure in the long run. Brye explained why he should work putting out forest fires for job security. At that time, there were numerous forest fires in the western part of Canada. Smoke must have invaded our city annually, but up until that time, I had never really noticed it all that much.

Well, he did apply. He quickly travelled out to British Columbia for an interview to see if he was a fit with everyone else. He heard back sooner than was expected that he was, indeed, a match. Conair Aerial Firefighting had an extra plane that year, and they needed an extra co-pilot. Brian would be flying a Convair 580 tanker, a converted passenger plane, dropping air retardant.

We flew out to B.C. on a date. Well, it was a house-hunting mission. True, we had a house being built back home prior to his job acceptance. But we had been waiting a long time to finally live in B.C. together. We found a home and made an offer, conditional on us selling our home in Edmonton. As we packed up our current home, we wrote love notes on every side of all the boxes. Brian loves Nettie. Nettie loves Brian. "I'll love you forever times infinity to the power of infinity." A line of love said for our entire marriage.

We thought our lives were set. He was so excited. I was, too. And... I wasn't. I hated the idea that we would be separated for an entire summer! And every year? You've got to be kidding me! I couldn't possibly make it that long without him.

(More of their signature embrace, photo taken by Brian)

How Do You Make the Journey Worthwhile?

1). How do you maintain the magic in your journey together?

a). Why bother? My spouse doesn't.

b). I celebrate Valentine's Day and anniversaries.

c). I pay attention to what makes them happy. I serve them in simple ways with no attachment to any reward.

2). How can I renew my loving feelings for my spouse?

a). I'm just putting in the time. Maybe they will try to make the love return.

b). I thought I was by telling them what they need to fix.

c). I think good thoughts about them. I notice and tell them what I appreciate in the everyday things they do.

3). If you're not married, must you stop believing that you, too, can have a happy ending, even if it's in the eternities?

a). I feel my happiness depends on getting married and sharing a life with someone, but it hasn't happened, and I am hurting. My time has passed and isn't coming back.

b). I usually have hope that one day—even in the far distant future—it could happen. It wavers back and forth.

c). I won't give up hope. I know my self-worth is not dependent on anyone or anything. My happy ending will come, in this life or the eternities.

TIPS

1). **Rock of faith.**

Be ready.

Find your faith and build it.

Yup, build your faith. When hard times come, that is not the time to prepare. Noah was commanded to build the ark when the skies were blue, not when it was already raining. I, personally, build my faith in God by reading my scriptures, meditating, going to church, praying on my own, as a couple and as a family.

Let me be very clear here. I have a personal relationship with my Savior, because I do those things. Also, I don't feel like I pray per se. I am a chatterbox all day! I do get on my knees to pray, but most of the time, my prayers are conversations with God. I know He has a sense of humor, because He can listen to me go on and on and on! I pray about the events of the day, I pray when a fire truck, police car, or ambulance go by. I pray for those serving to be safe and inspired how to help, I pray for angels to assist and bring peace to those who need help. So, if your loved one has passed by me in the cop car, or emergency vehicle, I have prayed for them. If your loved one needed their assistance, I prayed for them! I...pray...all...day! This, I feel, is why I get the answers I do get. I've invested my time in prayer when things are good, not just in the muck of it.

2). **Snuggle time.**

Snuggle time is the best. I didn't grow up with enough snuggles, so I cherish them. Adults need snuggle time just as much as kids do. Children need to see a wholesome, loving relationship between you.

Brye and I would take turns with each child. All four girls got snuggles at bedtime from both of us. (T.V. was not a priority.) We would tell the girls stories about our growing up. His were much happier stories than mine, and he would elaborate a little. Like the time he ate mushrooms from the yard and had to have his stomach pumped. He went on and on about how much he puked. The girls ate it up. Well, figuratively, that is. These stories are great for binding your family together. It can also rekindle wonderful feelings for your spouse; you may learn new things about them you hadn't heard before.

3). **Look.**

Look into their eyes! Look deep. See the speckles. See their soul. Love them from the inside out. Study their features. Love all their freckles, wrinkles, scars, crooked teeth. Love the way they wear their jeans, the way they breathe when they sleep, the way they lean to the side when they drive. No one is perfect. Love them for everything that makes them unique. Take the time to notice.

4). **Record it!**

Write down all the wonderful moments before time slips away. Add as many or as few details as you need. Get the good feelings in there. When Brian left, I read his journal. There wasn't much there, but what he wrote was all positive, wonderful life experiences. Catch it on video. No words can replicate the sound of your baby's precious laugh. Nor can you write exactly how he shaves his face. We have family videos of Brian in the bathroom, patiently allowing our daughter to hold on to his electric razor as he shaved. Precious memories.

5). **Love like you'll never get hurt**

So the saying goes. Don't live a life full of regrets. Good, wholesome, uplifting love should not be watered down. Love is healing. The times when I have given it my all are the times I also got the most out of my life. I'm no expert, but I do know that I don't regret when I have loved with all my being. If I could have been promised no pain in exchange for never experiencing the love I had with Brian, I would not take it. Even after knowing how much pain and suffering I went through, I would still endure it again. I know what love is. All the love I felt outweighs the pain. How can I say that? Because the pain is healing and leaving, while love continues to grow outward and upward.

(always close, always fun and always in love, picture by John Tilley)

Chapter 6

The End

It's funny the things that our memory can hold onto. There he was, I don't recall when, standing, looking out our bedroom window. "If I die, I want you to remarry, Nettie."

My answer was a sincere, "Uh, when I die, I *don't* want you to remarry. I couldn't stand to see you love someone else but me." Oh, my selfish pride.

"I'd want you to be happy and have someone to help look after the girls. You can't do it by yourself, Nettie." He knew I would still have no other family of my own to help. He was right. I couldn't do it alone.

I remember the last physical goodbye. He was about to leave. I prayed not to be in a feisty mood. I hated him being away, and I would get agitated. As we sat on the couch and held hands, I felt a spark between our fingers. The type of energy couples have when they first start dating. We were almost to our ten-year anniversary. The next morning, he packed up his things, including his mountain bike, hugged us tight, and kissed us all goodbye. Then, he said, "Be good for mommy, girls. I'll love you forever times infinity to the power of infinity." I didn't want to let go. Had I known for just how long until I would see him again, I would never have let him go.

(Classic Brian smile, picture taken by John Tilley)

Sure, we video called and emailed every day. We had family prayer together over these videos and phone calls. His emails were just as sweet as ever. When he said, "The smoke was so thick Nettie, I didn't know if we were ever going to get out," I was scared, but had faith he would be okay.

We were never able to celebrate our ten years together. He was away. He tried to exchange shifts with a fellow pilot, but someone higher up denied his request. He sent flowers. When I told the girls that Daddy sent me flowers, they were confused and said, "No, Mommy, some strange man gave them to you," referring to the delivery man. Brye thought that was funny. We spoke about him coming home for my birthday and our youngest's birthday in the weeks that followed.

Sunday evening, July 31, 2010, I went to my computer to see if Brye had emailed me yet. He had sent a work link to watch where his plane was flying. I opened it up. The planes were moving dots. His plane dot was not moving. I wanted to retire early, as I had responsibilities at the church the next day. I knelt down to pray.

Habitually, I prayed for the duration of our marriage to keep Brye safe from all harm. I prayed about his safety and our marriage constantly throughout the day. That evening, my prayer was different, odd, wrong. I didn't pray for his safety. It's like I forgot. Reflecting, I think Heavenly Father being a loving Father, hurt, not wanting to hear my pleas and not be able to fulfill them.

Brian's dad lived with us then. He had emphysema, but was still quite mobile. Our oldest daughter was working late at a restaurant at the mall. Grandpa had said he would pick her up from work for me. While driving home from the mall with our daughter, the radio on some random news station that Grandpa listened to spoke about a Conair plane going down. (Flight 448 Registration number C-FKFY). Grandpa was repeatedly following Brian's location. He, too, loved planes. That's when Amberly made him call and confirm if it was, indeed, Brian's plane. Amberly asked Grandpa, "Is that my Dad's plane?" Yes. It was.

When they got home, Grandpa must have been in shock and wouldn't come wake me to tell me. He didn't want her to wake and tell me either. Amberly, my young teenager of 15, was adamant that I be told. She opened my bedroom door to wake me, and said words that I will always remember, even though, as my journal recounts:

"She woke me with deepest cries of sorrow that were hard to decipher. I heard 'dead' and jumped up. I thought Grandpa was dead. He's been sick and not breathing well, (COPD). Before I got out of bed, I registered the words, "Dad's dead. Plane crash." I was up, shaking, pacing around the room, crying, not understanding."

My younger girls say I screamed a terrifying scream and woke them. I was hit. I sunk. I felt like this was a terrible nightmare, not really true. I tried to breathe. My world collapsed. I tried to be coherent. I felt my entire being shift. My mind, body, and spirit split in opposite directions. Nothing about me was aligned.

I went to my phone and called Brian. In my trauma-inflicted brain, I rationalized that Brye would answer and tell me that he was dead if it was true. Ironically, I was able to leave him a voice message, even though his phone was no more. My journal entry says: "I picked up the phone and called Brian to be sure. 'Brye. I love you. Tell me you're okay. Brian, I love you.' Over and over, I said this. I was crying hysterically, pacing everywhere. I was crying from my stomach. All my muscles were tight, from my stomach to my neck and face. It hurt so much."

Next, I redialed the last number on my phone. I had just happened to call a member of the Bishopric earlier that evening. This time, I wanted a priesthood blessing. I knew that God knew and would answer me in that blessing. Grandpa was still saying that there would be a rescue team. I wasn't about to wait. I trusted God's answer more than man's. Once I received the blessing, I became calm and could speak properly again, but I ached and felt confused. My heart was racing.

The girls and I somehow made our way downstairs to the front room. Heavy. I felt so heavy. My eight-year-old daughter, Savannah, suddenly shouted out, "I see Dad!" I whipped my head around to look out into the dark night sky, thinking this was all a mistake; that he was outside the house walking in. Then, just as quickly, my spirit corrected my mind. How could he be here when he was in British Columbia a few hours ago, flying? My heart sunk deeper. This is a bad dream. This can't be happening to me. I had had such a difficult life, and Brian was my miracle. No. Not me. Reasoning took over, and I decided to ask Savannah some questions. I knew little children can see things we cannot. I had to know everything I could.

"Where? Where do you see Daddy?"

She pointed in the corner of the room, not far from me. "There."

"What does he look like?" (I was so troubled that he had suffered, and needed confirmation that he was okay, even in death. Not that I really had any tangible idea of what this new existence meant for any of us).

"He's all white and glowing like the sun. I just see his head, no body."

"What is he doing?" I asked

"He's making faces." (Brye must have known how disturbed I was at this for sure.) She added, "He's making faces at you, so I will laugh. He doesn't want you to be sad."

Don't ask me why I asked this later, but I said, "Did he have his glasses on?", to which she replied "No."

I could feel him. I felt him standing in between the two couches that faced one another. I felt so much love and warmth. Brye and I had experienced immense love on earth, but this was far more intense than I knew was earthly possible. My heart was hot, as though on fire. In my mind, I could see my heart. It was crimson and appeared to be percolating, like tiny volcanoes were exploding all over it. To myself, I wondered if this was now his incredible loving feelings for me on the other side, since he could feel so much more without the containment of his body. I wrote in my journal, "The love I felt was an eternal love. The word and feeling *eternal* was strong. A first, I thought it was his love for me, but then, I thought it was my love for him. Now, I realize it was our love for each other." Immediately, a scripture came to my mind, "Hearts knit together in unity and love." (Mosiah 18:21) I cried more. Death could not separate our love for one another; only magnify it.

My physical eyes became dull as my spiritual eyes became enlightened. I saw him. He sat on the couch beside me. I could see a bright white being that felt like Brian. If I focused my eyes, he was out of sight. When I relaxed and allowed myself to see with my third eye, he was there. Maile came and sat down where he was. I assume now that he was just getting reacquainted with having no body, because he got up and moved over for her.

I know I got a priesthood blessing. I know people were there. I don't remember what else happened downstairs, but I somehow made my way back to my bedroom. I sat on Brian's edge of the bed. Somehow, I was now wearing his MEC fleece pants, socks, and favourite grey MEC sweater. I just had to feel close to him, to smell his scent on me.

Stammering for what felt like an eternity, which probably lasted one full minute, I sobbed out, (I really needed to know that he didn't suffer. I couldn't bear to think he had hurt in any way. Plus, I knew that he was in God's presence and could not lie to me.)

"Brian... d,d,d,d,d,d,d,d,d,d,d,d,d...did it hurt?"

"A little, but I'm okay."

I heard him. I heard him! Perhaps, I should have been more surprised in the moment, but it was so natural and peaceful. Contemplating afterwards, wow...what a precious gift from heaven for me! Hearing him felt so normal and soothing. Only when he left did I marvel at the moment.

How I slept, I don't know, probably from pure exhaustion amidst all the tears. It had rained so much for us that summer. I felt like the rain had been a foreshadow of the tears I would cry over the years to come.

Informing others. I waited as long as I could. I wanted to tell Brian's pilot friends what had happened, but I did not want to disturb their sleep. I knew how their schedules could be, and I wanted them to also be safe when they flew. By early morning, I was calling. It was such a difficult thing to actually verbally say, "My husband is dead." (Even to this day, I will run into someone who I haven't seen in years, and tell them the unfortunate news.)

Morning came. The warmth of the sun filled my bedroom and kissed my cheek. It was so welcoming after all the rain. I began to stretch and feel happy inside, until the reality of what had happened last night was not a dream, not some terrible nightmare. This was my new reality, and it punched me hard in my center. How dare the sun shine! Did it not know my world had fallen apart?

I lost weight like crazy in three days! I was 95 pounds wet. I didn't eat. I wouldn't drink. I felt like everything wonderful was gone and that I deserved nothing good in my life. Interestingly, people just kept bringing food, and lots of it. We had so many lasagnas that we are now not very fond of them! My breath was disgusting! I did manage to brush my teeth. I think I showered daily, but I can't be sure. I had to force myself out of bed. I wore Brian's clothes every day and night; the same clothes. The brethren and sisters (as we call everyone in the church) came to my aid. The women acted like mother hens, taking care of dishes and feeding my children. The men acted like protective big brothers. Parents from church and school took my girls on playdates. I could feel the strength of people's prayers; they started at 8 a.m. and ended at 5 p.m. That was an interesting experience. Priesthood blessings became my lifeline. I had people stay over at night in my front room for the first little while.

Help fizzled, as it does. Wonderful people get on with their lives as you still struggle, trying to make sense of it all. Time went by so fast and yet so slow. Roaming aimlessly around the house, time just creeped by, but after one week, I would be surprised, *What do you mean one week has passed since he died?* Time was not supposed to continue. Since my life had stopped, time should, therefore, also stop. I walked around and around the house. It felt like moments, but I think it was hours. Staring at the digital clock on my stove, the characters looked so unfamiliar, like a child learning how to read. I forgot how to tell time. Numbers and letters made no sense to me. My brain thought those things were unimportant as I struggled in my trauma. I tried to refocus my eyes, as though it was some sort of eye problem. Not making any sense of it, I returned to my continuous pacing. Something inside told me I should probably feed my children. I didn't know how anymore. Fumbling for the phone, I managed to call my visiting teacher. Crying, I pled for her to help me make lunch for my kids. By now, I think it was probably dinnertime. What a fog I was in.

Then, our dentist called. They wanted me to sign papers to verify the teeth they found were Brian's teeth. My Brian's teeth! I was horrified that his teeth were no longer in his beautiful body. No more smiling his handsome, crooked smile at me.

Then came his personal belongings from the hotel room. I searched everywhere for something—a note, something, anything to comfort me. His computer was there. It took some time before I could get my brain to work to remember the password. When I did, there were the computer post it notes we had written to each other. My *I love you's* and his, *I can't wait until I see you again and give you a big hug* notes. (I am still holding him to that promise.) I found his toothbrush and stared at it for the longest time. He had just used it. Now he was gone. Not real, not real, not real!

Planning a funeral- surreal. There were moments I thought I would just ask Brian what he wanted, and then reality would sink in. A friend recognized that I was in a coma-like state and began to take over the planning. Something inside me jolted awake, and I mustered the strength to do it. Friends and I rummaged through pictures to find the best ones of him. I chose hymns and speakers, the preparation list was long. Amazing Grace had to be played. It was *the* song of choice for funerals and I felt outside pressure to make everyone happy. However, it hadn't made it onto the programme. It just had to be played. And *voila*, just like that, Chris, a sweet friend felt my concern, and played "Amazing Grace" as our family walked to and from our seats.

Brian never made it to his funeral, not his body, anyway. I didn't have the heart to tell anyone, but maybe they already knew. Brian's body was being held up at the crash site. Transport Canada was investigating the crash site, and we had to wait to get him home. Out of the two pilots, Brian's torso was not completely consumed by the flames and was retrieved. A friend of ours, Bryce who owned his own body transportation business agreed to bring Brian home for us. He could feel Brian's spirit with him as he brought him home.

The girls and I climbed into the limo heading for the service. From where I sat, I was going backwards as we drove. That is exactly how I felt: my life was all messed up and speeding backwards. This was not my fairytale ending. The service had media attention—I think 500 people showed up. The local firemen came. They are so wonderful, the whole lot— there's a camaraderie between them, it didn't matter if you flew and put out fires, Brian had become one of them. They lined both sides of the front entrance in full uniform, sword blades lifted, as we solemnly walked underneath. I held my head high; I was so proud of my hero husband! He had saved people's homes and lives by his service.

I had asked everyone to wear his or her uniform. Police officers, firemen, even the bicycle couriers, arrived in their work dress. So many did. It was wonderful.

An empty urn sat forlornly on a table at the front. Beautiful, exotic flowers decorated the chapel, representing his many worldly travels. His body had not made it, but Brye was there. I could feel him sitting right beside me, with his arm around me. (I was so weak; he was probably helping me sit upright!)

Brian stayed seated beside us during the entire chapel service. I felt as calm and peaceful as one can under such circumstances. As the speakers spoke about how wonderful my Brye was, I felt like screaming to the world, especially to some people present, "See? I told you he was amazing!"

Afterwards, two of Brian's cousins were by my side, encouraging me to eat something and keep up my strength as I met, hugged, and spoke with every person who wanted to talk to me. I felt that I should bring them some comfort that they, too, were seeking.

Brye was there, comforting me. Somehow, the veil between this life and the next was thin for the girls and I at this time in our lives. Brian was at his service. I "saw" him. I could see him popping quickly in between people's conversations. He was happy. The feeling I got was that he was enjoying the stories people were telling about him, having a little chuckle, and that he really liked seeing everyone. That made me smile. I thought this would be my new reality. Could I get used to this? I loved having him so close, but hated that he wasn't really close; living in a different realm from me. But as wonderful as still having him around was, it didn't last. I had to become strong and move on. I didn't want to. I resisted.

After the service, the girls and I stepped out onto the church grounds.

The sun was warm. It was a beautiful day outside. The girls and I each had a white or silver balloon. Letting go of them symbolized so much. His last flight. His ascension into heaven. Letting go of the past. Letting him go. For my younger girls, it was just a fun activity.

In British Columbia, I was told that all the flags on provincial buildings were at half mast, in honour of Brian and the other pilot who died with Brian in that crash. I was so proud of him and so honoured by this token.

Another sweet token would be made later, on the side of the road for all to see the selfless sacrifice of these two men. Temporary crosses were at first erected. Those whose homes and lives were spared from what could have been catastrophic fire damage created a lovely memorial in their honor. I believe this was the Kanaka Bar Band. I am grateful that Brian's final sacrifice was recognized.

Next came the cremation. There wasn't very much left of him to bury, and I had no idea where to bury him. I wanted his body to remain with us. Then, when the girls needed to have a moment with Dad, they didn't need to drive to the cemetery. Plus, we were young; we hadn't planned to die anytime soon, so we hadn't made any arrangements.

Grandpa was with us. We pulled up next to a large cement building. The whole area looked like a large, disgusting, industrial part of town. Were we at the wrong address? Savannah's young memory remembers large, furnace-type doors. Inside was a tiny room, with a few places to sit. Someone had tried to make it look funeral home-ish, but it felt stony and stuffy. I still felt so disconnected to myself, to Brian, to my girls, to my life.

They brought us into another room. A cement room. Cramped and cold. There was a furnace and a box. A pine box with Brian's remains from the crash and the subsequent fire. In. That. Box. Their Daddy was...in...that...box! A lady in black gave us a few black Sharpies to write messages on *the box*! Grandpa was more a mess than I in that moment, I think. I felt Brian was there. I don't think I saw him, I just felt him. Brian was doing his best to comfort us. I knew that. I felt it. I think we were still connected. I didn't know how to feel. Brian was in that box, but Brye was with us. Spirit here. Body there. Separated. But still him. Crying, we wrote words of love to him. Someone (I don't recall if it was a man or a woman) said to take our time. Then, pointing to a very large, red button beside the furnace opening, instructed me to push it when ready. Brutal! I did not want to do that to him again! He had already crashed and burnt in the fire, why did I want to burn him again? But I had to; there was no escaping it. Grandpa couldn't do it (he was a mess), nor did he want to. I found my inner courage. I reached out and pushed that stupid, large, red button. Slowly, the pine box crept into the hot furnace with what remained of my beloved inside. My girls raced to my outstretched arms. We clenched each other as tightly as we could, and exploded into tears.

One day while driving my minivan and not long after the cremation, my four-year-old, my sweet, little Paige asked me, "Why did we have to push that red button, Mommy? And what happened to Daddy?" Stabbing pain again pierced my heart. After I answered her questions, she next innocently asked why frogs were green. Phew. I cried as she jabbered.

I was lifted, supported, and loved by friends, the church, and loving angels. Praying, screaming, crying, I pled with Heavenly Father. I knew I had a perfect marriage to a nearly perfect man, and it would be impossible to ever duplicate that. It would not be fair to anyone else. I asked Him to take away all feelings of being a woman, the need to be touched, held, and loved by a man. I would shut myself down and focus on being "Mom". I never wanted to love and get hurt again. Remember, I was 95 pounds, and had stopped eating. I felt I deserved nothing sweet or good in my life ever again. To keep me alive, people bought me Ensure drinks and almost forced me to drink them.

More troubles arise when you're in the thick of it, don't they? Most certainly. Because we were building a home, had an offer on a home, and owned a home - my life was complicated. When Brian took the new job, he cancelled his life insurance. It was expensive, due to his heart condition. Brian had assured me this new job had some life insurance. Well, when Brian filled out the home builder's insurance paperwork on the new home being built, he answered the questions/ticked off the box about taking it, but I guess he also checked off the "no" to insurance box. The *Bank* (oh how I really want to tell the world about my feelings for this *Bank*!) did not help a widow out. They denied me my home. So, the entire insurance we got from Conair went into paying for that home. Someone's heart must have been hardened. Would it not have been a simple write-off for a major bank? For a widow with four young kids, it would have made life so much easier. In a priesthood blessing, I was told that Heavenly Father was working on the person involved, but they had their agency. So, I do know the Spirit of God was working on them and *they* chose to say no anyway. Karma. That's all I am going to say about that. Karma.

(Brian's plane remains wrapped around the mountain trees, picture possibly taken by Neal McKinnon from Conair, https://bc.ctvnews.ca/mobile/air-tanker-pilots-killed-in-b-c-crash-identified-1.538167?cache=yesclipId104062?clipId=1723871)

The sound of sirens, the approaching fire trucks. I hated it all. I knew that rescue attempts had been held off due to the intensity of the fire. The crash had created its own new fire problem. A year later a crew member slipped up and told me that the sound of the crash was so loud and the impact was so intense...I couldn't bear to hear it. So, whenever a fire truck passed us, I would curl up inside and outwardly bawl. Movies had fires, and explosions, and airplane crashes...I would bury my head and cry. Leaving the theatre was always embarrassing—a light comedy with a crash scene, and I leave with swollen eyes.

The mail arrived with a package for me. Autopsy report. Did my horror never end?

Another package arrived in the mail. Transport Canada's report of the accident. I was to read it over, and then express my written opinion. Reading it was like watching the crash. Brutal. Someone was adamant that I give him/her a copy of the accident report. Law bound me not to. My name was transcribed on every page, so that if I were to make a copy, all fingers would point back at me. How much more did I have to endure? Wasn't losing him enough? Here I was, facing so much of this alone.

One day, I received notice that my time to make any written statement was drawing to a close. I bowed my head and prayed and prayed and prayed for help. I hadn't yet finished reading what they had sent. It was too much to bear. I sensed Brye was with me. Just the two of us. I could do this with him by my side. There were so many aviation terms that I got lost, but he walked me through. I know heaven was supporting me as I wrote up my statement with suggestions, that I have since learned are now practiced within his last company. This makes me smile. Knowing that Brian's last moments on earth created positive change for others.

My four little girls and I went bathing suit shopping at the mall (I had finally remembered how to drive). We found a bathing suit for one of the girls. Seeing as money had been rather tight for us, I picked up the phone to call Daddy and ask what he thought about how much I would be spending. What was I thinking? Why was I having such a hard time with this? Because it *is* hard, that's why. When you love someone as much as I loved him, grief is a reflection of how much you cared. I loved him deeply, therefore, I grieved just as deeply. In fact, I still have my moments. All of my dreams, like raising our family, my future with him after the kids had married, and all the plans we had made about being together were gone. If you have never gone through something like this, it is hard to explain. It's like living in a home and suddenly the foundation crashes, it disappears, and you're left with nothing but a crumbled mess.

Brian's dad, Grandpa, was still living downstairs. I loved him very much. He was my first real connection to a loving extended family. He loved spending time with us, and we loved being with him. He was full of laughter and not-so-funny jokes. He constantly took pictures of all of us and, then, enjoyed tweaking them on his computer, sometimes adding a bear or dolphin to the photo.

My friends had come over to comfort me, and we were talking when my cell phone rang. Grandpa was calling from downstairs. He told me he couldn't breathe. I immediately called 911. The paramedics whisked him into the ambulance, but didn't leave. They wouldn't tell me anything. Why weren't they leaving? The crew members just kept telling me that he was a very sick man. Finally, the lights flashed, and the siren sounded. Off he went. My mind was in too much shock at the time, so all I remember next is being at the hospital with Brian's extended family who lived close by in attendance. I prayed and then shouted in my prayer for Brian to get in there and make him well! I could not bear losing someone else I loved right now! Time passed, hours maybe, I don't know. I was in a fog of my own. He did recover and came home, but then he moved out shortly after. He left me when I moved on with my life. He did pass away a few years later, but I was never able to say goodbye.

(these two Tilley boys are now reunited, Brian and his dad, John Tilley, picture taken by unknown at Eden North Parachute School)

******

It took a lot of contemplation and prayer in deciding if I wanted to share these next spiritual experiences with you, the reader. In the end, I decided to treat you as honorable people. This is me being even more vulnerable, and sharing what I and my loved ones know to be true. Why? You ask. I believe it may be helpful for many. God is real. Those who are on the other side of the veil are not far, but here, so very close. Not everyone has these experiences. I understand that. I believe I have had these tender mercies of the Lord because I was all alone in the way of family support.

Driving home from church one Sunday, I could feel a presence in the van with us. I had been growing used to these wonderful feelings of comfort. I wondered if it was Brian, but dismissed the impression. When we got out of the van, I asked Paige who she was talking to. (Seeing as she had just turned four, speaking to herself was not uncommon.) She surprised me when she told me she had been playing peek-a-boo with Daddy on the ride home. I asked all my girls how church was and what they did. Paige again piped up and told me that Daddy was in her primary class, her Sunday school class colouring with her. My friend, Karen and I had walked past her little class that day and saw Paige with her hand on the chair beside her. I asked Paige about it, and she told me she had her hand on Daddy's leg. This brought me comfort. Since she was so small, of course she could see him. She probably saw him as though he was a real person. However, I told her that she wouldn't always be able to see Daddy in that way. In her sweet innocence, she looked at me like I was crazy! (Funny, how *not* seeing a dead person is crazy!) Oh, how I love my children!

My sweet Maile. She was six when her daddy died. Nighttime was hard for my children. While I was sleeping and having no dreams, due to the faithful prayers of others and daily priesthood blessings, (literally, I would wake up remembering white, just all white while I slept), my innocent children were having troubled sleep. I recorded this on August 17, 2010, "I remember the girls were crying/whimpering every 20 minutes or so with disturbed sleep. My friend, Tammy (who had stayed over to comfort us), had been checking on them while I slept. Each time she would get to the top of the stairs, their troubled cries would stop, and she would return to her spot where she slept on the couch. Maile woke up and looked into the hall from her bedroom. She saw a tall man with grey in his hair. He looked to the left and to the right, then, swinging his arm, marched down the stairs and disappeared."

When she got older she later explained, "I woke up, then I saw this man there, and I got kinda scared, thinking, uhh there's no men in this house. I pulled the covers up to my chin, so I could still see him. I felt safer doing this. He didn't smile, but he didn't frown, he was just looking at me. He took his arm and struck his right thigh, not like a salute, but like a 'soldier kind of thing'. He marched away. I waited, but I was curious, so I wanted to be sneaky and wait until he was downstairs and look over the staircase to see him. From my bedroom, I could see him take a step toward the stairs, but he didn't step down. Rather, it looked like he was walking straight out. When I went down to look for him, he wasn't there." My girls slept peacefully after his departure.

During my stinky days. The stinky days when I never ate and had breath that could make a mountain crumble. The stinky days I wore Brian's clothes—the same shirt, sweater, pants, and socks—day after day. The stinky days when I don't actually know if I showered. Those days. Those were my weakest days. People came to pay their regards at the beginning, and I took every opportunity to hear about or speak about Brian. I was standing in the front entrance way, listening to someone and felt my body fall backwards. I was alone, but I wasn't alone. Some being from heaven placed their hands on my back and gently pressed me forward and held me there.

My last goodbye. My friends from church came with me to the temple. I knew I would find great peace there. While seated with my eyes closed, I could "see" Brian in the other room. The beautiful Celestial room. He was leaning on a chair, simply getting to know other spirits that were also there, in his laid back, kind, and gentle manner. He was funny, too. I "sensed" him asking others how they had passed away! Who would have thought about a conversation like that! My heart was so excited to see him, even if in my mind's eye. I felt that Brian was seeing so much of this world in a more beautiful way.

My heart felt like it was pumping fast, but in truth, it was calm and quiet. (I placed my fingers on my throat to feel and be sure that it wasn't racing.) I felt peace. I wished I could feel this way all the time. My friends, Suzy and Kristie, sat on either side of me on the couch. With my head hanging low in contemplative prayer, I asked Heavenly Father if I was losing my mind because of all that I had seen and heard since Brye's accident. I am reminded of the quote from Harry Potter to Dumbledore:

> "Tell me one last thing," said Harry. "Is this real? Or has this been happening inside my head?"

"Of course it is happening inside your head, Harry, but why on earth should that mean that it is not real?" **J.K. Rowling, *Harry Potter and the Deathly Hallows***

I wondered where Brian was. I thought he might be in front of me. I prayed again. I remember saying, "I feel like Brian is standing right here, but am I going crazy?"

To which I heard, by the same voice that answers my prayers, "He is standing in front of you, staring at you."

I could feel Brye taking me in, memorizing me. The way he used to when alive. I opened my eyes. He was there. Unless you know what I am talking about, this may sound odd. He was there. I could see him, but not with my natural eyes. If I tried to focus on him, he was gone, but when I was unfocused and calm, he was there. I could see through him. He was dressed all in white: a white shirt, white tie, white pants, and white shoes.

I leaned forward, just in case I could feel him. I lifted my head, closed my eyes. I *needed* to feel him. I felt him drop to his knees and place his arms around my neck. Was he hugging me goodbye? I placed my head on his shoulder. That didn't feel right, so I switched shoulders. I knew he didn't have a body, but the tender mercies of the Lord made it so I could feel him. I snuggled my head into his neck, resting there. I could feel his neck by my face. I was turning my head and getting more comfortable. I felt so happy. We stayed like this for a while. He kept his arms wrapped around me and hugged me. I never wanted this moment to end. Inside, I had the distinct feeling that this was Heavenly Father's way of letting me say my last goodbye. Not that I would never see or feel him again, but just that I would not ever feel him in this form again. At least, not in this life. I was having my last hug, as though he were still in his body. Again, I know he had no body (I could see through him). It was a tender mercy. Brian then let go and "said" (his thoughts reaching mine), he had to go, I had the distinct feeling he was leaving to go comfort another family member. I felt he had to go see his mom, but I wasn't ready to let go. My spirit pled with him not to leave just yet. Suddenly, I felt him over by the door. He looked at me again. I felt his love. He wasn't in a hurry to go, but he had to go. He lingered a short while and left. He was gone.

So many people were kind to us. I received hundreds of emails and Facebook messages. I did my best to answer them all during my long, sleepless nights that followed.

PRIME MINISTER · PREMIER MINISTRE

August 3, 2010

The Tilley Family

Dear Tilley Family:

I was deeply saddened to learn of the passing of Brian Tilley in a tragic plane crash near Lytton on July 31. Laureen and I would like to extend our heartfelt condolences to you during this painful time.

Canadians across the country share your grief regarding this tragic accident, which occurred as Brian Tilley bravely battled the forest fires raging across the British Columbia Interior. While I know that there are no words to ease your sorrow, I hope that you will take pride in his noble and valiant efforts to protect the safety of his fellow citizens.

Please know that our thoughts and prayers are with you at this sad and difficult time.

Sincerely,

The Rt. Hon. Stephen Harper, P.C., M.P.
Prime Minister of Canada

August 3, 2010

To the Family of Brian Tilley
c/o Conair Group Inc.
1510 Tower Street
Abbotsford, B.C.
V2T 6H5

Dear Family of Brian Tilley:

Please accept my sincerest condolences for the loss of Brian. I can think of nothing more difficult to endure in life than the sudden unexpected passing of a loved one.

May you find comfort in knowing that Brian's work was very important to him and to all of us in British Columbia. He was an expert in his field. His determination and sacrifices really made a difference to our forests, communities, neighbourhoods and people. Our province is a better place and a safer place because of brave and courageous workers like Brian.

My thoughts are with you during this very difficult time.

Sincerely,

Gordon Campbell
Premier

Province of British Columbia
Office of the Premier
www.gov.bc.ca

#740, 999 Canada Place
Vancouver BC
V6C 3E1

August 9, 2010

Ms. Annette Tilley

Dear Ms. Annette Tilley:

It was with great sadness that I learned of the aircraft accident that took your husband's life. I want to extend my personal condolences and those of the BC Forest Service. We were all deeply saddened to hear of your great loss.

All the dedicated men and women, who work in the Wildfire Management Branch, and those across the ministry supporting our wildfire operations, are deeply impacted by the loss of Brian. Brian was well respected by his colleagues and an experienced pilot who was an integral part of the wildfire fighting team. Several of my staff have taken the time to share with me stories of their valued interactions with Brian.

It is difficult to express the deep sense of gratitude that all British Columbians have for those who dedicate their lives to the preservation of our safety, fire season after fire season. We are indebted to Brian who bravely faced the risks associated with the unforgiving wildland fire environment to keep our homes, our families and our communities safe.

Our thoughts and prayers are with you, and your children during this very difficult time. May you find comfort and strength in your memories of Brian.

My Deepest Sympathy,

Dana Hayden
Deputy Minister

Ministry of Forests and Range Office of the Deputy Minister Mailing Address: PO BOX 9525 Stn Prov Govt Victoria, BC V8W 9K2 Tel: (250) 356-5012 Fax: (250) 953-3687 Website: gov.bc.ca/for

The Prime Minister and his wife sent me out a personal signed letter. The Premier of British Columbia and the Deputy Minister of British Columbia also sent us letters. Others whose homes were saved sent cards and notes, and many sent cards of condolences. My home had been listed for sale. The realtor asked if I was still selling, then came by, removed the sign, and handed me a check. Friends from my girls' school, neighbourhood, and church bought school supplies, took my girls for the day, took care of my lawn, brought us copious amounts of food, and cleaned my house. I even had a friend's husband mop my floor.

A trust fund was set up, and so many generous people donated their money to help us out. The generosity touched my heart. People, strangers, cared about me and my children.

A sweet lady from church arranged a hotel stay, so the girls and I could escape the media, the constant visits, and telephone calls for one night. The hotel was super sweet and let us stay for free.

We felt Brian's presence with us, comforting us, guiding us, and sometimes just hanging out with us as we struggled to move forward in life. Sometimes, I would laugh how I could get used to this. I "saw" him more now than when he took the new job. Not everyone appreciated my humor.

How Do You Move on When a Chapter Has Closed?

1). When you feel broken in every way, what do you do?

- a). I become depressed and think about suicide. Life will never get better.
- b). I stay angry and blame the world, because it motivates me to get out of bed and complain.
- c). I pray. I ask for help. I believe things will get better. I take one step at a time, even if that means simply brushing my teeth.

2). When traumatic thoughts sweep over you, how do you combat them?

- a). I am too weak. I listen to it, cry and feel sad/anxious/depressed. I like people to feel sorry for me.
- b). I push it down. No one can see I hurt. I smile for everyone else.

c). I recognize it. I give it a name, and I change my thoughts to, "I am strong and this will make me stronger."

3). How do you not stay mad at God when bad things happen?

a). I am angry. I am simply moving through the motions of life, waiting for time to heal all things, and maybe one day I won't be angry. As I do nothing to resolve this anger though, I feel it grow. As it grows, I get sick...

b). I don't trust Him anymore. I just don't care. I dedicate all my energy to others' needs and forget about healing myself and my relationship with Him.

c). I pray again and again. I fast, read scripture, meditate...I ask Him what my next step is. I face the storm, I hurt during it. I will learn what I need to learn, knowing when I get out, I will help someone else through their similar storm. That keeps all things in perspective, so that I will not be or stay mad at HIM.

TIPS

1). **The pain is real, and it will pass.**

So far, I have skimmed the surface to tell you my story. It hurt more than I care to explain. I felt as though I could barely take a breath. Whether it's my story or whether it's your story, our pain is real. It cannot be wished away. We have to go through our own trials and challenges.

I found when I held pain in, it festered and got worse. My advice is: let the waves of grief flow through you. You will learn how to help someone else through your suffering. The storms will calm, then rise again, and calm, until they truly start to settle. Knowing this is normal may be of help to you. You are normal. The universe is not out to get you. I believe God trusts your strength and is making you stronger. He needs strong warriors in His kingdom. I know with Him, you will be stronger sooner than doing it on your own.

2). **People will say dumb things.**

The first time I went to the grocery store after the accident, I habitually made my way down the deodorant aisle. I stopped, staring at the men's deodorants. I would never buy deodorant for Brian again. I began to weep. Then, I began to ugly face cry. I had been alone until a familiar face came towards me. She gave me a much-appreciated hug, but she also told me not to cry. Not here in the store. I told her, yes, yes I could cry. I just lost my husband, and I didn't care if anyone saw me grieving. I'm sure she meant well, and I don't hold any negative feelings for her.

After a year, I went to my doctor and told her I was feeling depressed. She asked if I was still grieving. I told her I was. She left the office and returned with a book. She pointed to a place on the page and told me it said I should not be grieving after a year. I never went back to her.

People just don't know how you are feeling, unless they have experienced something similar. Sometimes, they try to compare. Sometimes, they try to console. When they say words like, "Time will heal all things" and "It'll get better with time", remember they mean well. Now is not the time to be angry with those who mean well. Let it go.

The very, very best comfort I received was from one of my Sunday school primary children from church. He was about ten years old. A shy, quiet soul. Without saying a word, he meekly approached me and gave me a loving hug. Then, he simply walked away. Perfect. Words aren't always necessary.

3). **Cry.**

You don't have to cry in the grocery store, but let it out. Cry in your room, cry in the car (pull over first!). Cry. Cry. Cry. You're not showing any strength if you end up sick and miserable because you held it in.

I cried so hard that eventually the tears would not come, the ugly cry face was still happening, the pain was still intense, but my body would not make one more tear. And then, the ugly cry face began to settle. The tears dried up for a time. But every now and then, they will still slip down my cheek. It's okay. We are human. We have tears for a reason. To let the pain and stress escape.

4). **Talk about them.**

Talk about them or talk to them. They are still close by, most especially after their passing. If you cannot see or hear or feel them, that doesn't mean they aren't near, comforting you. You are cared for. Talking about them (or having a conversation with them/to them) is such a wonderful process. Tell them everything you would if you *could* see them. Why not? What more do you have to lose? They are so very close. There were times I could see Brian ready to comfort a family member, but they would not. They were in such a state of grief that their hearts were hard. If only they had said a prayer, asking for help, they would have felt (or maybe even seen, who am I to know?) him there comforting them.

Talking about Brian keeps him close to me. He is my eternal husband, how could I simply forget him? Talking about him has become such a part of our everyday lives that it is not taboo to say his name. I have felt him close as I wrote this book. My children know who he is from the memories I've shared. They better understand what traits came from him: their patience and loving nature, their odd sense of humor, the way they grind their teeth. I feel it's important for them to still feel they have a connection to their dad. He is a part of them.

Talking heals wounds.

houghts.

I believe there's a fraction of a moment in time just before you process a thought. For example, I saw a plane in the sky, it registered as "normal" at first, but then this mini thought came in that said, *You must always look up at the planes and remember Brian, remember he died and be sad. People expect you to stay sad.* So, I did.

I believe there's these mini thoughts that give us an immediate choice. It's so fleeting, you have to catch it. But that is where the ultimate freedom of choice lies. We can take it. I didn't for the longest time. I let the loud, painful thoughts take powerful control far too often. I should have listened to the mini, healing, positive thoughts from the start. Instead of making the trauma worse.

6). **REALLY take care of you.**

You must take care of you. Healing doesn't typically fully happen overnight. As human beings, we heal in layers. It's a process.

Yes, depression and anger set in for me. I didn't listen to those mini thoughts and allowed explosive thoughts of anger and resentment right into my heart. Why me? Why am I always punished? Why does God not love me? Why does He love _____ more than me? Yeah. Not good. And so not true. You go through your trials for a reason beyond what you can comprehend. A very personal reason. I believe it's not just for a generic "To make you stronger" type of reason, which is a legitimate reason for sure, but it's more than that. You have a purpose. Going through tough stuff is part of that purpose.

I heard all the self-help speakers say to be positive and think positive and great things will come. These positive thoughts did not stick. They rolled away like water on a duck's back. I did not believe them. If they are not sticking for you either, find out why! Be persistent.

Keep trying. Keep getting help. Personally, I was tired of feeling this way and didn't want to drag out the healing process any longer. I tried Rapid Eye Movement therapy, hypnotherapy, psychologists, yoga, meditation, exercise, food therapy, therapeutic touch, energy therapy, magnetic therapy, naturopaths, bioenergetic therapy...I was determined *not* to be a victim of my circumstances anymore.

You can do it. Just do something. Move forward. Be believing. You are always stronger than you give yourself credit for.

Chapter 7

The New Beginning

More was asked of me. I hadn't even gotten used to this new extreme reality, and my faith was tried even more. More on top of the death of my husband and best friend, more than telling everyone he had passed, or the world seeing his destroyed plane on the news, or pushing the big red cremation button, or selling our house, or not having enough money, or family feuding, or reading the autopsy report, or even reading the report from Transport Canada and writing a statement. The trials testing my faith kept coming. Through much prayer and what most of the world would say is an impossible, revelatory event I was informed...

Well, let's just slow down and catch our breath for a moment. Take a seat, and I'll tell you.

My August 18th journal entry: "After only a couple of days after the accident, I kept getting a name (no first name) pressed into my head of a man. I would pray and loudly speak to Brye, "No! Get that name out of my head! It is not funny. I don't want to remarry. Make me strong, so I won't need a man. Take away all the feelings of any kind of physical need." Then, I would sob and sob.

My August 23rd journal entry: "I prayed about 'the Name' I got. I kept... well, within the first few days, for almost two weeks, I kept getting Donna's name - but with her son, Kevin, as an impression in my mind. (I couldn't remember his name, and the one time he came to give me a blessing, I introduced him as Dennis, his Dad!) I prayed again tonight and got the distinct impression: *You will marry him.* I wanted to know who the impressions came from- Heavenly Father or some other source. I will pray about this again, of course, and, then, I will ask the Lord Jesus Christ and my Heavenly Father if Brye could come for a visit and 'discuss' this with me! ... My memories of Brian are sometimes painful. I am missing my Brye and the companionship we enjoyed. There will never be another quite the same."

This same Donna from church had made a quilt to comfort me after the accident. She left it with me, explaining she wanted to give it to me right away, but that the binding was still left undone. She would return and fix it. So, I left it in the gift bag she brought it in, at the top of the stairs, on top of our little keyboard. One day, shortly after Brian's passing, sometime around when the impressions had come, I lifted the bag to move it elsewhere. Brian's spirit was beside me. Let me tell you, when someone dies, they are still the same person they were in this life. Brian liked to make me laugh and smile. He thought he was pretty funny, and if I got mad, he'd do something silly, hug, or tickle me, until the corners of my mouth lifted in a grin. Today was no different. But I *did not* like what he had to say and the corners of my mouth *did not* lift into a grin. With my hand clasped around the handle of the gift bag, I heard him say in a sing song voice, "There's your future mother-in-law!" Maybe you can understand—you know the moments when you are so mad at your husband that you want him to leave the room? But you don't really want him to leave, because you aren't finished getting mad at him yet? Well, that was me.

My August 25th journal entry: "My prayer today 'Does Brian approve of Kevin?' 'Yes. He does. He wants you to be happy.' 'When will Kevin be more a part of our lives?' 'At the end of ...year' (Hmmm, what year? A year from the accident or end of this year?) Oh boy... I think of Brian...I miss him every night."

I also saw Kevin in my dreams; I saw his eyes, really saw them. They were sweet, and my spirit felt they were like the gentle eyes of the Savior. When I had had priesthood blessings, I would still wake up feeling as though all I had dreamt of was pure white. Just white. When the frequency of priesthood blessings stopped, my dreams at first were nightmares, which tossed me back and forth. The nightmare would lift, and I would see Kevin's face. Feeling this was not right, I forced myself to think of Brian and the nightmare would begin again, only to suddenly switch into a new dream of Kevin and both his and my children playing together in the ocean. Needless to say, on those nights, I slept so poorly, struggling with what was being revealed to me.

My August 29th journal entry (four weeks after the accident): "Last night I prayed for sweet dreams, either about Brian or Kevin. I had a dream...Kevin was asleep. He woke up and I saw his face vividly. His eyes were soft and gentle."

I knew from prayers and the answer was clear. I hardly knew *him*. I was furious. I was hurt. I felt abandoned. I defiantly said something to the effect of, "Well, if this is what you want, then please have Brian show him how to properly date me and love me."

Another August 29th entry: "Okay, so at church, I was constantly thinking about K.T. Why does my mind do that? I was even giddy. What is going on? Kevin often looks like he is napping in church. I kept thinking, 'Wake up!' He turned around once and seemed to do a double take! When he left, he seemed to take a short pause just beside me, changed his mind, and carried on. What is the deal with me?"

My journal continues with witness after witness of friends who were also being *worked on*. Four ladies immediately had the impression that Kevin was to be my next husband. I was simply interested in a friendship and not wanting to rush anything. I felt this wasn't *my* plan. My plans had just been destroyed. All the while, Kevin was still in his sleeping stupor, although my friends said they thought he knew something was up.

I have to tell you that things were not all that rosy, even when you are veiled in heavenly help. Driving, I would cry so terribly that I was an accident on wheels. I didn't care. I hoped I would be called back home to be with Brye. On one such occasion, as I was driving, probably with sobbing breath, snotty tears, and ugly cry face (side note- those kind of cries really tighten the skin under the chin!), my cheeks suddenly got very, very hot. I am not one to blush very easily, usually not at all. But, I knew Brian did. His cheeks would get very flushed. I touched my cheek and asked out loud if this was Brian's way of telling me he was near. My cheeks grew hotter. I knew this would be my "tell". To this day, he makes the cheeks of my family burn to let them know he cares about them and that he is close.

I knew I had a heart that could love and bring happiness to another, but I begged the Lord to take away all the tender feelings that couples experience, to strengthen me, so that I could once again be a single mom and make it all on my own. Unbeknownst to me, I needed to relearn how to love and trust. Too many "trusted loved ones" had hurt me in my past, and left me, either intentionally or not, as was the case with Brian dying. This time, I had four young girls. The oldest was fifteen and the youngest was three when he passed. I needed to realize how much these precious girls needed me. I yearned for more reasons to live. They would grow up and leave. I had to know I still had a purpose and that there was something more for me to do. What was it?

I didn't tell my girls this revelatory secret right away. Brethren in the church were stopping in to check on me every morning and evening with their wives or family to give me blessings. Kevin came, too. Once with his daughter and once without. (You've got to realize, these men had not had time to explain in detail what they had said to one another, so that the next person could repeat it. Every one of those blessings were individualized, revelatory, and sacred.) However, one day, a friend gave me a blessing from Heavenly Father, and he mentioned me marrying another man. Afterwards, he profusely apologized and said he just felt that was what he had to say. He seemed surprised when I told him I already knew and had known for some time now. The secret was out. I had, of course, told my best girlfriend.

Soon several more friends, including the men, got these *feelings* that I was going to marry Kevin. Some heard Brian's voice, and others felt his presence in our home. More confirmation. I know Brian was watching over us. After all, we were still his little family.

I wasn't just submissive, calm, and peaceful. I had temper tantrums. Fits of shouting out my anger to God for taking away My Miracle!

My August 29th journal entry: "Last night (after yelling at God), I felt like Brye was trying to comfort me, but held back, because in my head, I kept screaming 'Go away!' I was so mad, but I never really wanted him to go away."

In the end, I knew deep inside that Heavenly Father and His Son loved me and wanted what was best, so I turned most of my stubborn will over to His. Trusting things would somehow, someday be better than this. I was what you could call a sassy obedient child.

My August 31st journal entry: "I prayed before bed to have dreams. I dreamt of Kevin and his children... I awoke, prayed, and slept again. Each time, I know I dreamt of Kevin...I think I am either happy or excited about a happy future with him. I don't think of anyone else like that... If I am not happy... I am filled with guilt at having thoughts of anyone but my Brye. One cannot control one's dreams, can they? I find myself excited to see Kevin, and then guilt and sorrow, for I do so miss my Brye so much, and if I had a choice, I would be with him. Since I have such a long time before I see him again, is it wrong for me to see a possible future with Kevin? I'd like to go walking with him. Maybe Brian could come, so I would know he was watching over me, protecting me, and, perhaps, approving of this future?"

I need to mention these important details. When Kevin and his daughter, Jade, came with flowers after Brian's passing (the first time he had ever visited me at my house), he thought for sure he had known Brian when he was a youth. I explained that Brian would not have known him or hung out with any Latter -Day Saints when he was young, because he did not join the church until he was 26. Kevin was perplexed. In his heart, he truly felt they knew each other, besides the casual greetings at church when Brian was alive.

Here's the other detail: as I was showering, I could feel Brian was on the other side of the curtain, so I began a conversation. (Those were hard times, when I knew he was there, yet I could not always see him, and I wanted him to really be there! I wanted to reach out and hold him so badly!) Brian could have travelled the entire world and back to find me a new husband, so I asked him, "Why Kevin?" Brian answered me as clear as day, "Because we were friends." I knew immediately what he meant- they had been friends before this life.

My September 3rd journal entry: "Paige wanted to go to the park. We had already gone out delivering flyers that day, so I did not want to go out again, but I went anyway. After the park, I felt like I should go see Donna, Kevin's mom. Actually, I was *very* impressed that I should go. (I had a staple gun I had borrowed, so I could return it.) I prayed that I would not tell her ANYTHING! This impression came into my mind: 'You don't have to be reserved with Donna.' Wow! The topic came up about who would be in my future. She said something about it being her son! She told me I had been the topic of discussion when her entire family had been at the lake for summer holidays. Needless to say, I told her lots. I told her about the dreams, the answers to my prayers, how others were getting impressions about the two of us, about Brian's closeness to us since his passing, the last goodbye in the temple, and how Brian said he and Kevin were friends. I still haven't spoken to Kevin about... anything! Not a word."

My September 8th journal entry: My girls and I were at the church, because they had Activity Days for the young ones and had youth group for my oldest. Amberly, Savannah, and Maile were playing in the gym, and little Paige wanted to tag along. I don't know why, but I prayed for Kevin to show up at the church. Lo and behold, who walks in the very door where I am standing? Kevin. Funny thing;

I had only recently looked up his first name! Brian and Kevin had shared a teaching responsibility in the church. Whenever Brian had to leave unexpectedly to go flying, he would pass the handbook over to 'Bro. Tidball', and Kevin would teach the children for him, a tag team teaching thing. I was serving in the primary (children ages 2-11) as a councillor, and only knew him as Bro. Tidball, too.

Anyhow, I digress. In walks Kevin. My mind and body were not on the same page. My mind was uninterested, but my body was flirting, and what came out of my mouth was *not* what I was thinking. I would say, who knows what now, in a flirty little way (okay, maybe it wasn't that bad), and, then, my mind would argue and say things like, *What did you say that for? Knock it off. You are acting stupid!* Then some other little giggle would escape. *Say whaaat?* I was embarrassing myself. I had never spoken much to this guy before. The conversation was...comfortable. I asked him about himself, and he opened up about his recent heartache. I spoke openly about Brian. It was...nice. It was...easy. I didn't have to be reserved.

What makes this even more odd is that I could feel Brian's presence beside me. My cheeks were burning (he was encouraging this). Talk about the weirdest feeling ever! You could say that I was blushing if you want to, and I suppose I was inwardly, but my girls could feel Brian there, too. It is the weirdest experience when your deceased husband is beside you, watching you flirt, and you know he has hand chosen the other man beside you to be your future companion and father figure to raise your girls. Whenever Brye was close, I was relaxed and flirting. When he left, I would argue, argue, argue. It was really a battle!

Eight-year-old Savannah came running to me, with Maile and Paige close behind. Savannah, who is typically the speaker for the three of them, piped up how she felt like there were angels in the gym, playing with them. She knew Daddy was close, because her cheeks kept getting hot, but mentioned that he kept having to leave. (This makes me laugh even to this day, knowing he had to keep going back to keep an eye on me and make sure things with Kevin worked out.) Even in the minivan on the way home, Amberly said she finally felt her cheeks get hot, too! She hesitantly confessed she also felt that way on the way *to* the church."

School was starting, and I needed help with the city bus schedule and getting my eldest from her early seminary lessons at the church (which ran weekday mornings before school) to her new high school. Before Kevin left the church that night, he offered to help me "take care of it". He gave me his phone number and told me to call him late that evening, but I refuse to call guys first. I offered him my number and told him to call me, instead. He looked confused, but agreed.

After all the girls were asleep, I lay down in my empty bed, now sleeping only on Brian's side (something I have continued to do to this day), and my phone rang. It was about ten at night. People didn't really call all that much anymore, and not that late at night. I picked up the phone to hear a sweet, sheepish, unsteady voice say, "Hi. This is Kevin. Kevin Tidball." I hadn't been away from him for more than an hour, maybe an hour-and-a-half! How could I forget who he was? He was strong, cute, and funny. Oh, how I smiled to myself. Who else would be calling me at this hour, and how many Kevins did he think would be calling me? I didn't know this then, but I do now: Kevin is not an overly chatty person, especially on the phone. This time was different. I think Brian was showing him how to date me!

My children were also strangely comfortable with Kevin. Savannah wanted to spend more time with him, and Paige (who spoke to no one) would grab his hand and start talking as they walked. Maile and Paige would climb up and get shoulder rides. Kevin was always a gentleman, thoughtful, cautious and respectful. The girls and I spoke about Brian openly around Kevin and his two children, because Brian was still an active part of our family, and Kevin was fine with that.

On September 15th, we met again at the church for our children's youth group. Nothing very romantic, I am afraid. He asked if I wanted to come with him to fill up his truck. Inside, I screamed *absolutely no*, but of course, my mouth sweetly said *sure*! After filling his tank, I told him I had something I wanted to say to him. (He confessed afterwards that he thought I was stopping things before they started. If he had only known the struggle I was facing!)

I wanted to be obedient to Heavenly Father's plan, but I also thought I could scare Kevin away, and if he left, well...I had done my part, right? Being obedient in my own feisty way. We drove and parked the truck on the side of the road. This is how I remember the conversation:

"My very best friend, who I trust more than anyone in the entire world, has told me I have to marry you! I'm too old to play games, so do you want to start dating now or wait or what?" I'm pretty sure I said "or what", sassy-like. (I had just turned 36 a month prior! Wow, I was so old!)

Come on, Kevin! I was giving him every opportunity to run for the hills! Crazy lady here! Stay away! But, no. That is not what he did. He surprised me. He frustrated me and surprised me, softening my heart just a little. He clearly was unaffected by my widow-gone-wild behaviour and said, "If I can't be a friend to you now, what good am I?" And that was that. He really did have tender eyes and a gentle spirit.

He would come by to visit. It was the weirdest feeling. I felt like I was married and cheating, but I wasn't. He was there, sitting on the couch. Sitting beside him, I suddenly just saw his hands. The rest of him was blurry, and all I saw were his hands. From his hands, his wrists then came into view, and his arms. I don't understand it, and I have no explanation other than I was awakening to a new man in my life, piece by piece. My trauma mind could handle only small sections of change at a time.

We started to spend time together. We'd go on walks with my four and his two kids. He'd take me on his Ducati motorbike. Except for holding onto him on the bike, we didn't touch. Each night, I'd cry myself to sleep. Not knowing if Brian was always around to hear my complaints, I'd still talk to him anyway. Explaining how I felt like I was cheating on him. Crying about how others were treating me. But being with Kevin felt so natural and so comfortable. The battle was raging inside of me. Because of Kevin appearing so suddenly in my life, family members treated me poorly, and friends stopped talking to me altogether. Neighbours would shout insults as they passed. I was judged so harshly. They had no idea the torment I was going through.

Somewhere along the way, we started to plan for the future. Getting married.

My sweet six-year-old, Maile. So full of faith. On October 7th, she said she prayed and asked if, "Mommy could marry Kevin." She then went on to tell me, "I had a warm feeling about it. I was a little bit hot. It was right in my heart, and, then, it was kinda like he touched my heart. I felt good. And, then, I knew it was for really right."

I didn't take off my wedding rings, and did so very reluctantly, until Kevin came to pick me up to go ring shopping. Crying. Staring at them. Remembering when Brye proposed and they fell through the stairs. I gave them a gentle tug. The doorbell rang. I stuck my finger in my mouth and wiggled them free. I felt naked without them. I can't actually explain the hurt and betrayal I felt.

Kevin and I went twice with no success to look at rings. On the third try, I prayed and brazenly said (like you'll see I did about the entire wedding planning), "If this is what you want, then You (meaning God) and Brian will have to make this work! I'll get married, but that's it!" On the third try, I placed a beautiful ring on my finger. Kevin saw the brief look of joy sweep over my face. He immediately shouted, "We'll take it!"

The same comments proceeded shopping for the wedding dress. Every single one I tried on looked amazing! When does that happen? Inside, I just didn't care. I was grieving, not celebrating. My heart was sore. I chose the one that was the cheapest—a couple hundred dollars, including the fitting with the seamstress!

We were planning on getting married right away. I knew this was what was right. He must have also known. Why wait? It wasn't quite the same as "when you know, you know" as I had with Brian, but I still knew. We decided the coming January would work best to be married.

As for location, Kevin suggested we marry in Mexico. I spent most of the morning calling places only to be politely laughed at. Didn't I know I had to book a year in advance? So, again, I prayed. *Look, I didn't want this. You guys please sort this out, or I am done*! Immediately, Kevin called me and suggested we get married in Hawaii. (I had no family that wanted to come, so changing the destination was no problem. None of my friends could make it, either. I would be alone with my girls and a family I hardly knew in a strange place I had never been before.) "Sure," I said. "Good idea." Again, I "spoke" to Brian and the heavens. *Look, you guys, I am not having fun doing this. If you want this to happen, I need more help than this*. And wouldn't you know it? The first place I called had a spot! It was so *Brian* in all the details. The man who booked us and married us was a balding hippie man named Captain H. (The Captain of a ship...?) He wore a sarong and a Buddhist shirt to marry us!

We flew there. I hadn't been on a plane, obviously, since before the crash. It was brutal. I clenched the arm rests and cried the entire time, thinking only of Brian's last flight: his take off and his last crash landing. All the *whys* filling my head. Why him? Why me? Why did he go up without the man he trained with? Why was the alternator fixed on the plane? Why? Why? Why? Flying was not something I wanted to do ever again!

We settled into a beautiful house we rented, so all of Kevin's family could join us and some of his friends. It was lovely. The weather was gorgeous. We had a swimming pool and were steps from a private beach. You'd think I would be happy. I was grieving. If I was healed, I would have basked in the magical moment. Not everyone gets married on a beach in Hawaii! I could barely breathe. I faked a smile. I knew I cared for Kevin, and I knew I could love him. I knew this was right, but I was seriously struggling. I felt like I was the only one feeling this way, except perhaps Amberly, she was old enough to feel the hurt of losing two fathers in her young life.

The eve before the wedding, I lay on my bed crying. My girls were there, but they were young and having fun. They didn't understand. I had no family. Kevin's family hardly knew me. No one wanted to talk to me. Many people had said terrible things to me and behind my back about me getting married. I knew what I knew. I knew this was the Lord's will, and that nothing they said would change that. I had no friends here. I felt terrible, and was so very, very alone. I prayed again, begging Him not to make me do this. My answer was that He had not *made* me do it. I had had my free agency the entire time. But that was not how I felt. Wasn't this supposed to be like a fairytale, a dream come true? (Literally, it was...I was getting married on the beach in Hawaii!) Soon, there was a knock at the door. Kevin. He somehow knew to come. He brought his family to comfort me. We were all strangers. It was difficult.

Morning dawned. In the dark hours of the early morning, Kevin and I took a limo to the location. It began to rain. Then, it began to downpour! Everyone in Hawaii would tell you that rain on your wedding day is a sign of great blessings. My girls' hair and dresses were soaked when they arrived.

I sat in the hair/makeup artist's chair. He made my hair look amazing. It was beautifully curled and pinned up with blossoms of plumeria. He asked me how I wanted my eyelashes, did I want the elaborate falsies? I didn't know the difference, and I didn't care. I was trying not to cry off the mascara. I ended up looking so overdone. Okay, then I kind of cared, but was too worn out to say anything. Regretfully now, I wish I had!

The Captain came in and remarked how calm I was that it was storming out, and how this didn't seem to affect me. He mentioned how other brides-to-be get all Godzilla-like if it rains, as if he can control the weather. (I was hoping the wedding would get cancelled.) Inside, I was a terrible mess. The storm broke briefly, and we were able to get some photos done onsite and at the beach.

I put on my happy face, and even felt some happiness during the photos. It was surreal. It felt like I was acting for the camera.

We headed indoors for the ceremony, since the rains had returned. By now, our children, his family, and his friends had arrived. Braden was dressed to match his dad: khaki pants and a wet white shirt. Our girls looked beaten. (The way I felt.) They had worked so hard on curling their hair, but it was ruined from the torrential rain. We said our vows. What I had written came from a place deep within my heart, so that was real to me. Captain H. took out a conch shell and blew that thing for what seemed like hours! He explained that the longer the conch rang out represented how many years we would be happily married. I didn't know it then, and it took several years to accept it, but he was right, and mother nature had blessed us, too.

(Kevin, Captain "H" and Annette. Married in Oahu, picture taken by unknown)

(Kevin and Braden in Oahu for the wedding. Picture taken by Donna Tidball)

(The new "Tidley" clan as we became known as - Tilley + Tidball =Tidley, picture by Donna Tidball)

(Blowing of the conch, Oahu, picture taken by unknown)

(Storm clouds passing, wedding day in Oahu, picture taken by unknown)

We both had no idea what we were stepping into. I was hurting all the time and very unkind. Kevin wasn't Brian. This was not okay with me. Everything hurt. People were so unkind. But he was patient. I cried myself to sleep for months. He held me. I sank into darkness, and he stood there with his hands outstretched, offering to pull me up. He would come home, and I would be curled up in a fetal position on the floor, holding Brian's urn in both hands, screaming, crying, weeping, wailing. I may have been there for hours. He coaxed me and held me tight. I would take the longest showers. I felt it was the safest place to cry and no one would know, but Kevin knew. We would take the kids to the park. I would swing on the swings so high. You know when you have pumped your legs so much that the swing has met its match? It reaches the top and then drops down. I would swing and be in this odd state, just trying to figure out how crashing must have felt for Brian. Kevin would sadly watch me, and when I was done, he would hold me once again. He still wasn't Brian. He would never be. But, man, I needed him; more than I understood. Kevin is a fantastic man with a very gentle, loving heart.

Kevin and I had a disagreement. (Actually, I brought on many disagreements.) The bottom line: he wasn't Brian. He didn't look like Brian, he didn't sound like Brian, he didn't speak like Brian, he didn't smell like Brian, and he didn't love me in the *exact* same way that Brian did. I took off in my car. I did NOT want to be married ANYMORE to ANYBODY! Tears were streaming down my face; my vision was blurry, and I was hot with anger and so much hurt...and then there was Brye. My cheeks burned. (They had to, I guess, in order for me to pay attention.) I sensed him close. Then, I saw him and heard his voice. He was in the back seat, in the middle, leaning forward in between the front two seats. I heard his spirit speak to mine.

He said, "Go back."

What?! Was he serious? He was my eternal companion! My forever husband. Couldn't he see how much pain I was in because he wasn't here and I married a non-Brian? I shouted at him! I complained to him!

He peacefully, calmly, and quietly said again, "Go back." I sobbed and screamed some more!

"Whose team are you on?" I asked. "You are supposed to be on *my* team, not his! What is this? You are on *his* side?"

He just kept calmly repeating, "Go back." Eventually, I caved and whipped my car around, heading home, because Brye said so, and even though I was furious with him, I loved him, I trusted him, and I must have known he was right. I needed Kevin more than I cared to admit.

I still wasn't the only one sensing Brian's presence. My children could "tell" when he was around, and then check with me—were *my* cheeks burning? One day, the girls and I had music playing, and we were having a good time, just like old times. We were dancing around and laughing in the kitchen. Kevin had just gotten home from work, and was sitting on a chair. He was smiling and watching us. Kevin motioned for me to come over, and whispered in my ear that he felt that Brian was there with us, that he could feel him smiling and knew he was happy that we were happy, which made me all the happier.

When someone dies, they don't stop loving you, and you don't stop loving them. It is nothing like a divorce, with the falling out of love, betrayal, and all the baggage that goes along with it. Your heart breaks in a different way. It's like a piece of your heart is missing, and until you are reunited again, it will always be a hole. Explaining this to my children, I said it was similar to when people lose a limb. They still feel as if it's there, and it will always be missing, until the resurrection, when their limb is reunited with them again. However, my heart was stretching. Even with the empty hole, it was stretching and making more room for me to love more people.

An off-handed comment was made about how I should not have so many pictures of Brian in my house, especially a wedding picture. I needed to move on and forget him. I was married to Kevin now. I told Kevin how I felt. Kevin has always accepted that Brian was part of our entire family. He cares and watches over all of us, not just me and our girls, but *all* of us. Kevin is an exceptional man. He gets this. And because he gets this, I love him all the more for it. Digging into boxes in the garage, Kevin returned with a large, framed picture. It was my wedding picture to Brian! He placed it in our living room, right beside the urn. Talk about a confident man!

I would say by the time we had been married three years would have been a good time to start dating Kevin. By the time we had been married five years, I recognized that I loved him, and by seven years, I knew he was my new best friend. I say that, but the truth is, when God puts people together, when He is in charge, it somehow all works out. I needed Kevin sooner than that though, and so did my girls. We needed to be loved and supported. I needed a family. I needed someone to love me through the hardest time of my life. My girls love him, and I love my new children that came with Kevin. We are a family.

When God puts a family together like that, it has a higher chance of survival. Everyone has their free agency to make choices, of course. Our family merged fairly easily. I now had a new son and daughter, Braden and Jade. Our children got along, our extended family got along. We had some hiccups, sure, but life was and is good.

Years have gone by. Most of the pain has lifted, but some pain can pop up with little triggers. I've learned how to overcome. I've learned how to trust my instincts and to trust God. I've learned how to quiet the dark voices in my head and let in Light and truth. It is a process. Yes, indeed, time can make life struggles better, but I truly feel one has to actively make the choice to heal oneself and work toward becoming who they were meant to become. Find your true inner self. If you are not challenged, you don't grow. And was I ever challenged!

Like the moment so long ago...Brian staring out the window, commenting on how he wanted me to marry again if anything were to happen to him. How he wanted someone to be there for me and the girls. Essentially, through all of this, he said, "I want you to live."

And...I want *you* to live!

Do You Believe in Yourself and New Beginnings?

1). When the world thinks you're crazy, but you know you are right, what do you do?

a). I stop telling people my plans and reconsider what they said. They must be right.

b). I must be crazy. What was I thinking?

c). I remind myself that I know what I know, and they can't take that away from me. I will attract new people who support me.

2). What do you do when doubt creeps back in?

a). I let it. Nothing has worked out for me so far.

b). My plans are too difficult. I'm not strong enough. I quit.

c). I re-read my journal. I remember how I felt when I first knew. I keep moving forward, even if sometimes it's slow. I'll get there eventually.

3). Who do you seek approval from when it seems the world is against you?

a). Why would the world be against me?

b). I do my best to be unnoticed, so that this can never happen. I can't imagine how terrible that would feel. I wouldn't have the strength to face any opposition. I don't like any sort of confrontation.

c). I get a little rocky at first, until I relocate my footing. I remember who I am, that life is a journey, not to be complicated. I remember what my end goal is and stay focused.

TIPS

1). **Goosebumps**

Of course, I realize how unique my story seems to the outside world. Of course, I realize not all people will believe I saw what I saw. It depends where they are in their journey of life. I do tend to ask those who have a faith system to pray about what I have said, to get their own witness. Funny, isn't it, how whenever I tell elements of my life's story, people will say, "Ooh, I just got goosebumps." I believe goosebumps are an indication that you should pay attention.

2). **The plan.**

I know. I keep mentioning *The Plan*. Well, there is a plan. It's not written in stone every detail of your life. But, the most important details, the ones that will shape who you become, will happen. One way or another, you will get the hands-on training you need to specifically become the great person you are meant to become. Life is going to send you *lessons*. My advice is to not make life harder than it has to be. Pray, meditate, find your true inner voice that will lead you. If you know something is wrong to begin with, stay away from it. No one gets a detailed itinerary of their life's events, but we can get a step-by-step guide from time to time. Someone greater than us is out there, willing to help us in our journey. Call it the Universe, I call it God.

3). **More than the eye can behold.**

I'm not the first, nor will I be the last, to speak of Heavenly things. I was blessed to be able to learn what I did when I did. I know from years of prayers and spiritual insight that I was meant to share my story with you. It's not an accident that you are reading this. There is so much more to this life than we know. There is so much more in the life to come.

4). **More than one witness.**

This was a very devastating moment in my life and the lives of my children, not to mention all the grief felt by his family, friends, and those who loved him. My desire is to give them and all of you comfort, knowing there is so much more to this life. There is a life after death.

At times when I thought I was crazy—because in this world of people who don't understand, that is what they say... crazy. But, it wasn't just me. There were others who quickly got their own witness. I am so grateful that there were so many others who had dreams and visions, saw, heard, and felt Brian, and all that was heavenly in our home at that time of great tragedy. I am comforted by this verse (and others in the scriptures):

2 Corinthians 13:1 "In the mouth of two or three witnesses shall every word be established."

5). **You be you.**

It was my inner spirit that connected with Brian's spirit. It was my inner being, my inner me that connected to those spiritual moments. It was my inner being that shook me to realize Brian was not alive and outside my window when I heard my daughter say she saw Daddy. It was my inner me that would wake me from my stupor to focus on the funeral planning and get it done. It was not my mind or my body in control in those moments. They were falling apart. It was my spirit that held it all together and found beauty, love, and joy in the darkness.

Over my life's journey, I have grown more and more in tune with my true inner self. This real me. This stronger, more confident me. This happy, positive, courageous me. This person lives deep inside all of us, desiring us to focus on truth and be in control of our bodies and our minds. This is the real YOU. And this is a never-ending journey. I believe this is one of the greatest works we can do.

Recognize your true being and become the TRUEST, PUREST YOU that you were meant to become.

(Three months before Brian passed away - look how the Savior seems to be calling him home! Picture taken by unknown)

(A temporary memorial was made at the side of the road, and one year after the crash, each girl wrote a sweet note to Daddy)

(Annette and girls, so much sadness. Memorial site near crash site. Picture taken by Kevin Tidball)

(Kevin and Annette on honeymoon, picture taken by shuttle driver)

(Kevin and Annette in Montana picture taken by Kelsey Sharpe)

(Kevin and Annette selfie)

(The "Tidley's" from left to right, Braden and wife Magi, Maile, Savannah, Kevin, Annette, Jade with husband Jake, Paige, Amberly with husband Craig and son Arlo. Taken by Kensey Dee Photography)

About the Author

She got the news while fast asleep. Accident. Her young daughter's stammering voice, "Dad's dead." Forest fires. Fatal plane crash. Four young girls. Widowed. Despair. A heart-wrenching scream escaped her mouth. Life would never be the same. Her perfect husband gone. Her life felt over.

Annette Tidball is no stranger to the trials and tests of life. Having experienced great adversity of her own and feeling discouraged and full of despair from these difficult life challenges, she has developed a sensitivity which enables her to be empathetic towards others.

Instead of crumbling when her foundation was shaken and then destroyed, Annette has maintained an enthusiasm for life which draws others to her and her message of love, hope, endurance, and faith. Annette shines light on the dark events of life and exposes truth in an uplifting way. Not only does she exude courage; she sparks a flame of courage within.

Those who know her know she loves dancing with her sweetheart (at weddings and Christmas parties, as well as in the kitchen and local convenience stores) and singing in the car. And she says with a smile, "No lip-syncing in my car! If you don't know the words, make them up!"

She experiences the most joy spending time with her strong, tender-hearted husband and their family of six children. However, Annette continues to not act her age. Besides enjoying her daily yoga routine, she loves being adventurous with her family enjoying paddleboarding, kayaking, wakeboarding, hiking, snowboarding in the Rocky Mountains, and whatever new challenge comes along. She is continuously learning new things and lives by her motto, "You don't have to be perfect to be great!"

As Annette reminds us, when you lose someone, they are not lost. Love is never lost or forgotten. A memory is not tarnished when you live and love again. True love is inclusive. True love has no boundaries. True love is sacrifice.

Instagram : @annettetidballofficial

email: support@annettetidball.com